iBIBLE

VOLUME 2

The Great Flood (Parts 1 & 2) + The Tower of Babel

www.i.BIBLE

iBIBLE Storybook Volume 2
Copyright 2022 by RevelationMedia, LLC

Published by RevelationMedia, LLC
PO Box 850005
Richardson, Texas 75085

All rights reserved. No part of this publication may be reproduced, stored in a retrieval system, or transmitted in any form or by any means electronic, mechanical, photocopy, recording or otherwise without prior permission of the publisher, except as provided for by USA copyright law.

All Scripture quotations, unless otherwise indicated, are taken from the Holy Bible, New International Version®, NIV®. Copyright ©1973, 1978, 1984, 2011 by Biblica, Inc.™ Used by permission of Zondervan. All rights reserved worldwide. www.zondervan.com The "NIV" and "New International Version" are trademarks registered in the United States Patent and Trademark Office by Biblica, Inc.™

Executive Editor: Steve Cleary
Creative Director: Andrea Wilson
Copy Editor: Lisa Cooper
Designer: Mark Belin
Images From: iBIBLE. Created and Distributed by RevelationMedia (www.RevelationMedia.com)
Distributed by RevelationMedia (www.RevelationMedia.com)

www.i.BIBLE
#iBIBLE

ISBN: 978-0-9992893-9-6

Printed in China

Presented to:

_____

From:

_____

May the story in these pages, the one Divine narrative, bring you closer to the One who keeps His promises, who set His rainbow in the clouds as a sign of His covenant with all of creation, and calls you by name.

How beautiful upon the mountains

are the feet of him who brings good news,

who publishes peace,

who brings good news of happiness,

who publishes salvation,

who says to Zion,

"Your God reigns."

—Isaiah 52:7 [ESV]

CHAPTER 4:

The Great Flood (Part 1)

It came to pass, as mankind began to multiply on the earth, the sons of God saw that the daughters of men were attractive. And they took wives for themselves as they pleased. And the LORD God said:

GOD: *My Spirit will not live in man forever, for they are flesh; therefore, their lifespan shall be 120 years.*

THE GREAT FLOOD (PART 1)

And in those days, the Nephilim were on the earth. These were mighty men of old, men of renown.

THE GREAT FLOOD (PART 1)

And God saw that the people on earth were very wicked. The intentions of their hearts were only evil. And God regretted that He had created mankind.

GOD: *I will destroy mankind, whom I have created, from the face of the earth, both man and beast, and everything that creeps, and the birds of the air, for I am sorry that I ever made them.*

THE GREAT FLOOD (PART 1) 10

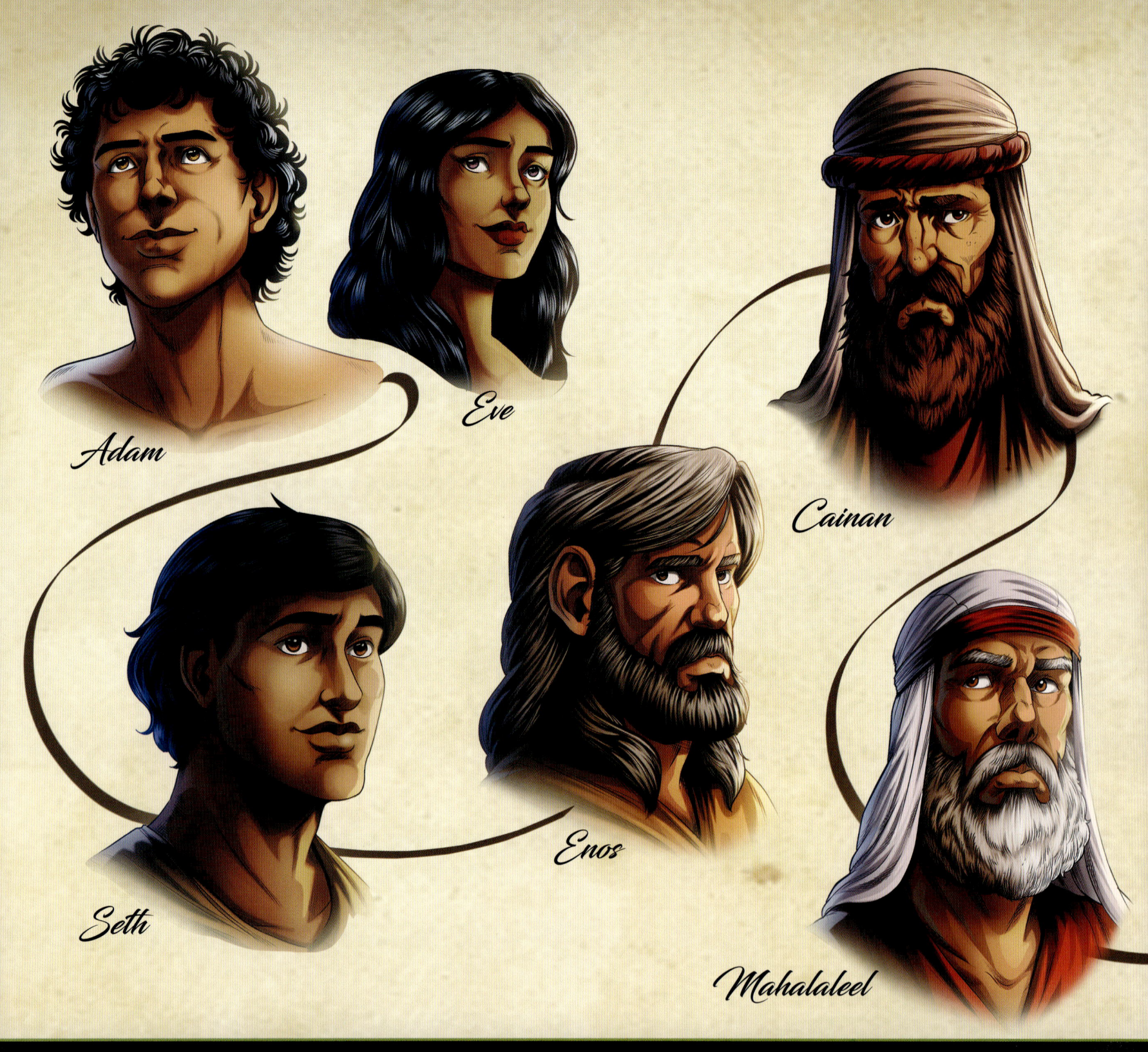

Among all the wicked people of the earth, there was a man who found favor with the LORD God. His name was Noah, and

He was a direct descendant of Seth through eight generations: Enos, Cainan, Mahalaleel, Jared, Enoch, Methuselah, and Lamech, whose son was Noah.

THE GREAT FLOOD (PART 1)

Noah had three sons named Shem, Ham, and Japheth.

THE GREAT FLOOD (PART 1) 15

And God spoke to Noah:

GOD: *The earth is filled with violence. Because of this, I will destroy that which I have created.*

THE GREAT FLOOD (PART 1) | 16

GOD: *Make for yourself and your family an ark of gopher wood. The length of the ark shall be 300 cubits wide and 30 cubits high. It shall contain three levels, and within each level you shall make rooms.*

GOD: *At the top of the ark, you shall make a window, and in its side a door. Then you will cover the ark with pitch inside and out.*

THE GREAT FLOOD (PART 1) | 20

GOD: *For behold, I myself will cause the waters to flood the earth and destroy every man and beast under heaven.*

Yet, I will establish My promise with you, for I have seen that you are not given to wickedness like other men. You are righteous before Me and those around you.

You will enter the ark along with your wife, your sons, and your sons' wives, and you only shall be saved.

THE GREAT FLOOD (PART 1)

GOD: *Of every living creature you shall gather, of every kind of livestock, wild beast, and creature that crawls, and you shall bring them into the ark.*

You shall take seven of each clean animal, a male and its mate, and two of each of the unclean animals, a male and its mate.

THE GREAT FLOOD (PART 1) | 25

GOD: *And you will take seven of each kind of bird, a male and its mate, and keep them all alive with you and your family to repopulate the earth.*

GOD: *And you shall gather enough food for your family and for all the animals.*

Noah did just as God had commanded him.

And when Noah was 600 years old, he entered the ark with his sons, his wife, and his sons' wives.

And all of the animals that were gathered together entered two by two; male and female alike, and then the LORD God closed the door of the ark.

THE GREAT FLOOD (PART 1) 33

After seven days, the fountains of the earth burst, and the windows of heaven opened, and it rained on the earth for forty days and forty nights.

THE GREAT FLOOD (PART 1) 35

As the waters grew higher, the ark lifted and floated on its surface.

The water overpowered the earth, covering the highest mountains by 15 cubits.

All living things that dwelled on the earth perished.

Only Noah was left, along with those who were with him in the ark.

THE GREAT FLOOD (PART 1) 36

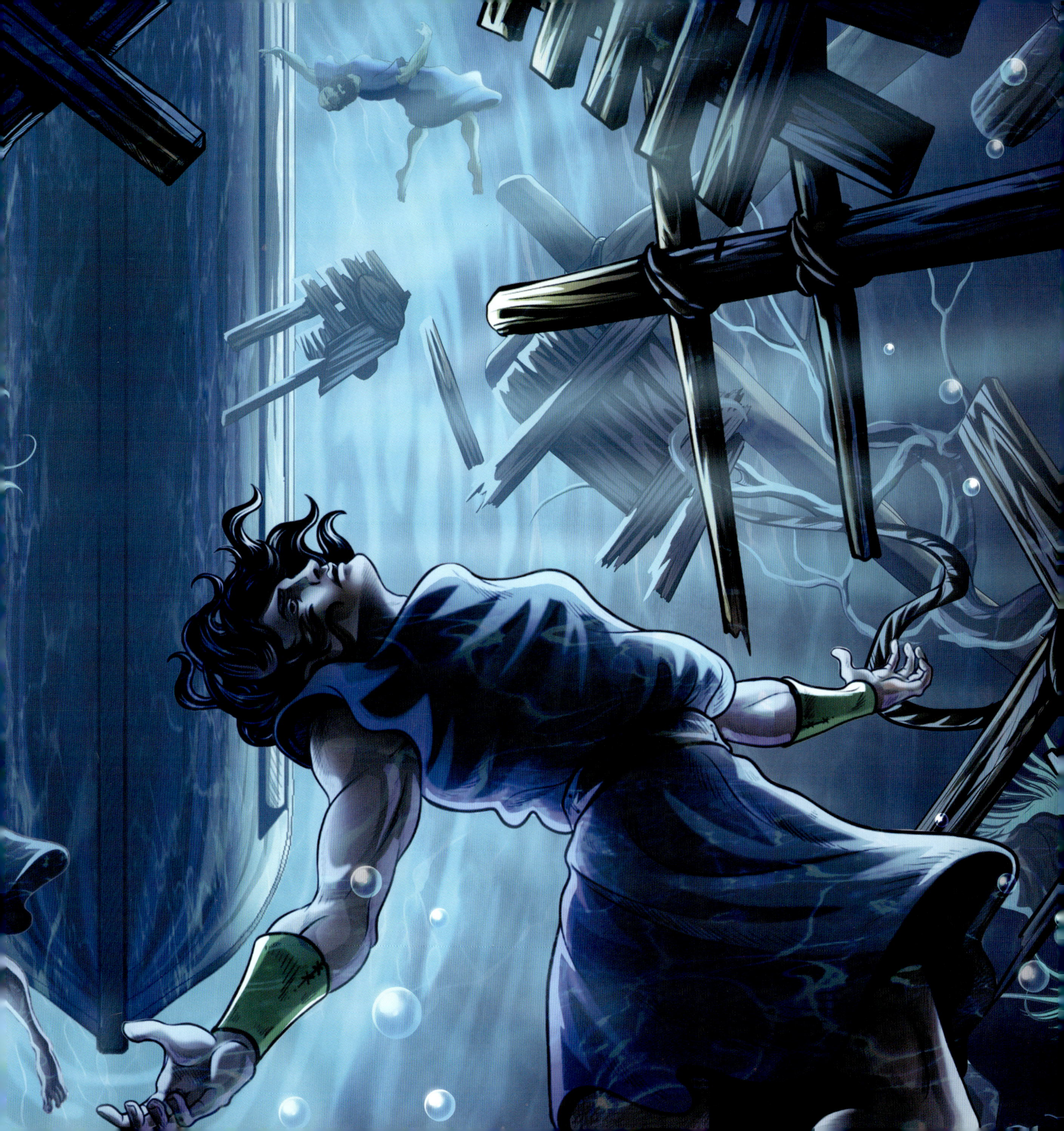

Chapter 4: Key Scriptures

God saw how corrupt the earth had become, for all the people on earth had corrupted their ways. So God said to Noah, "I am going to put an end to all people, for the earth is filled with violence because of them. I am surely going to destroy both them and the earth."

In the six hundredth year of Noah's life, on the seventeenth day of the second month—on that day all the springs of the great deep burst forth, and the floodgates of the heavens were opened. And rain fell on the earth forty days and forty nights.

—Genesis 6:12–13; 7:11–12

WATCH CHAPTER 4

CHAPTER 5:

The Great Flood (Part 2)

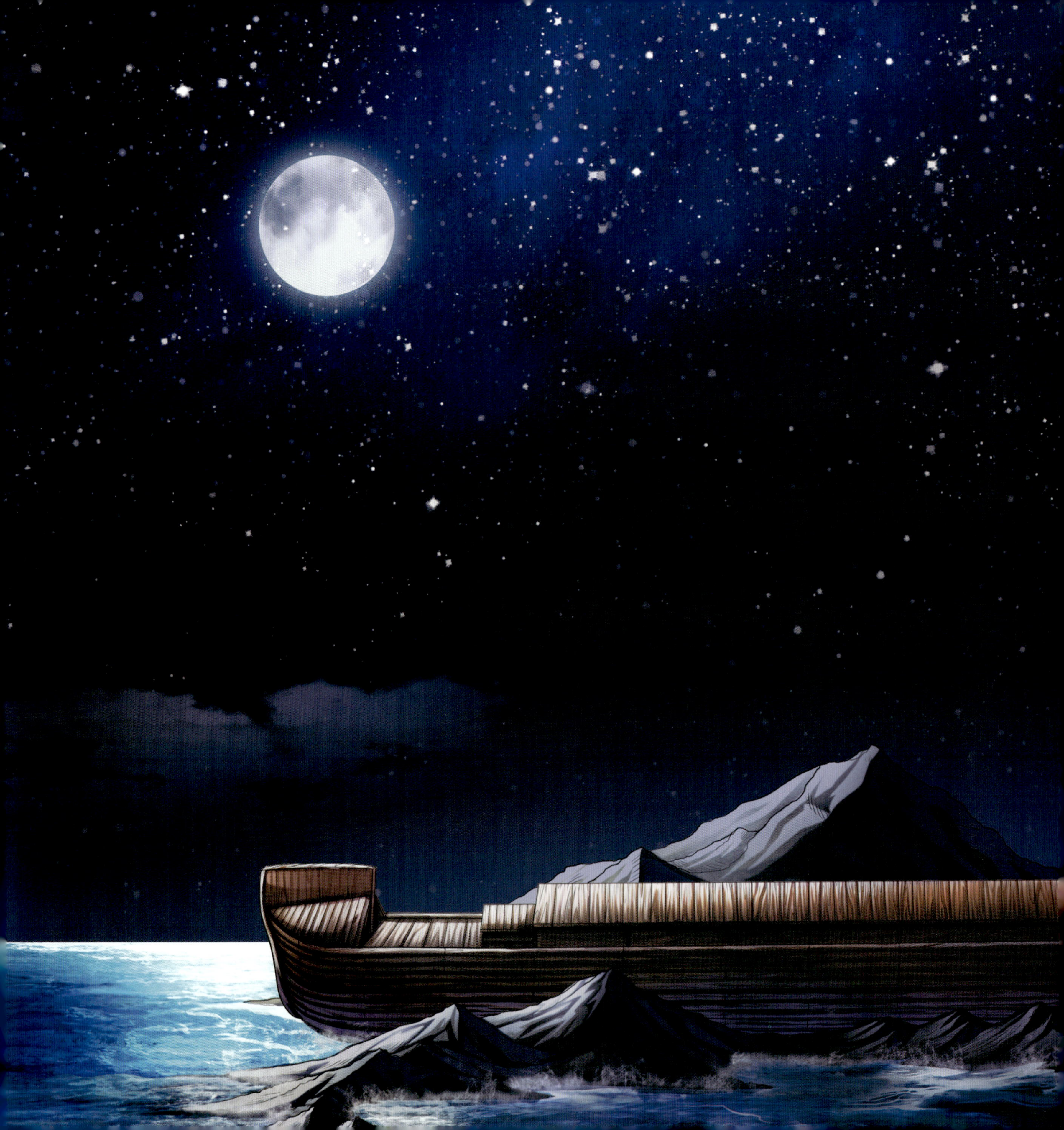

God remembered Noah and all the animals in the ark and made a wind to blow over the earth, and the waters began to recede.

And 150 days from the time the flood began, the ark came to rest upon the mountains of Ararat.

The waters continued to subside, and soon other mountain tops were visible.

THE GREAT FLOOD (PART 2)

After another 40 days, Noah opened the window at the top of the ark and released a raven, which flew back and forth until the waters had dried up.

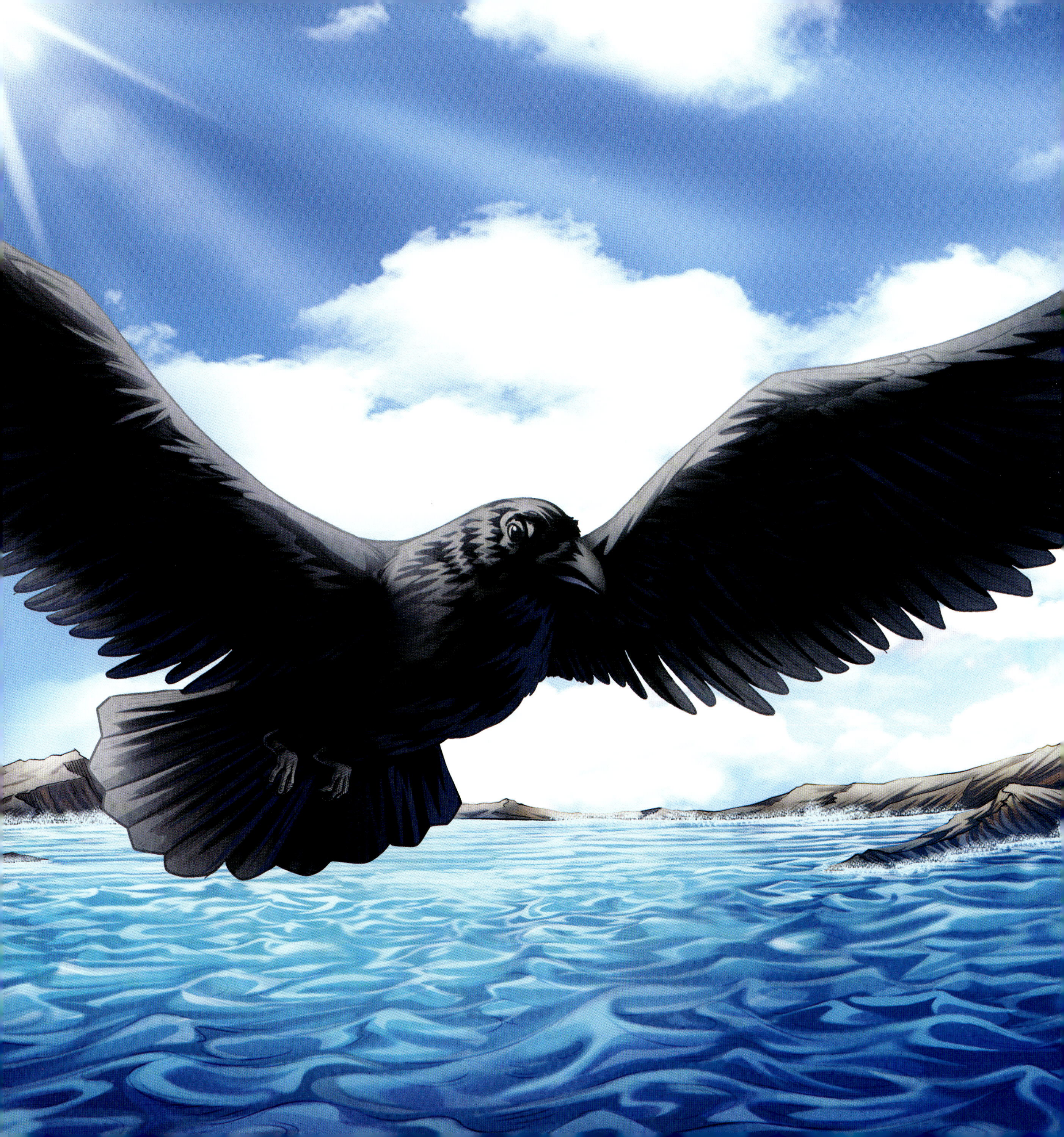

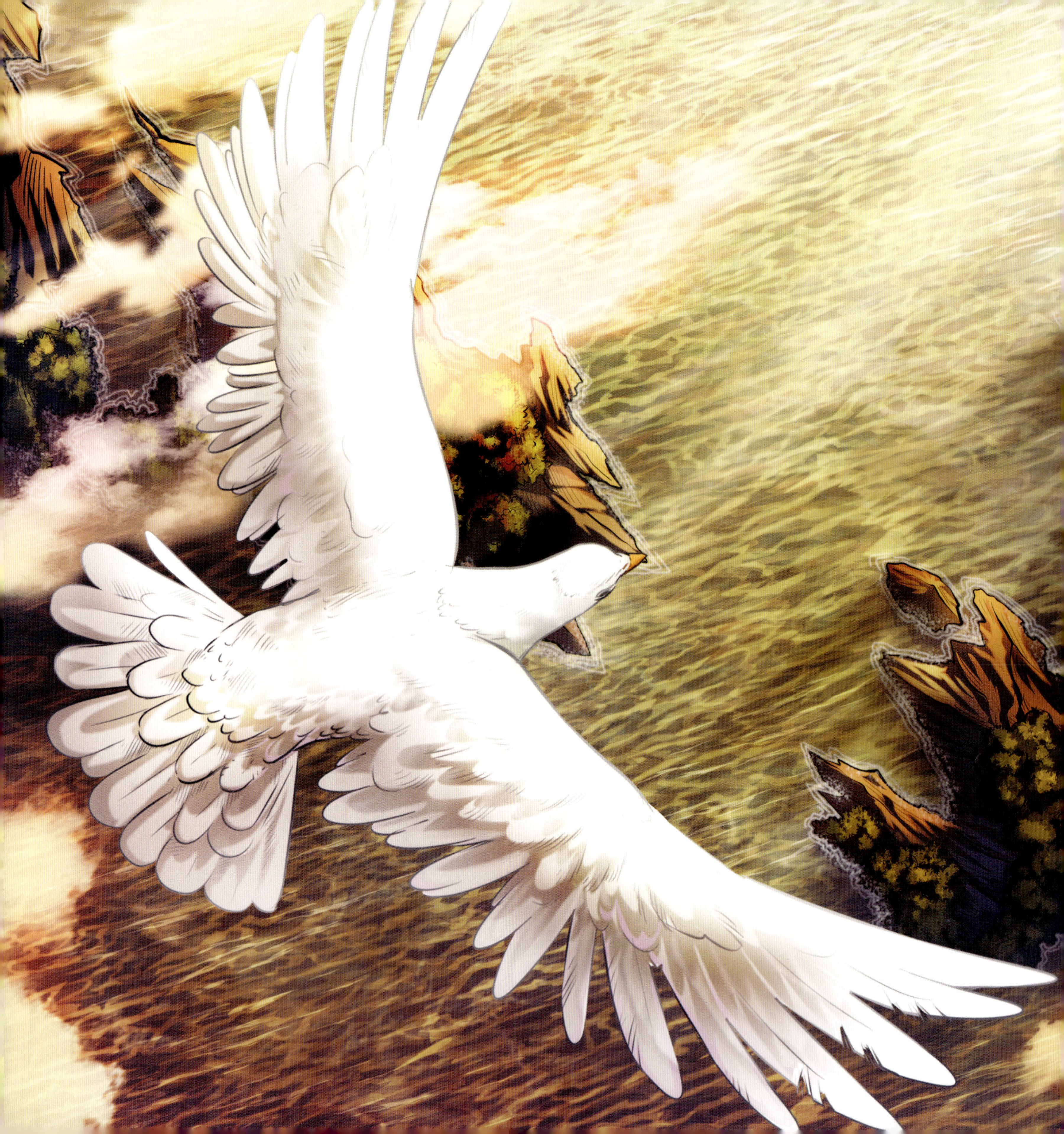

Then Noah sent out a dove to see if the waters had subsided, but the dove found no place to rest her feet and returned to the ark. So, Noah brought the dove safely back into the ark with him.

THE GREAT FLOOD (PART 2)

Noah waited another seven days and again released the dove.

And that evening, the dove returned to Noah, and in her mouth was a freshly plucked olive leaf.

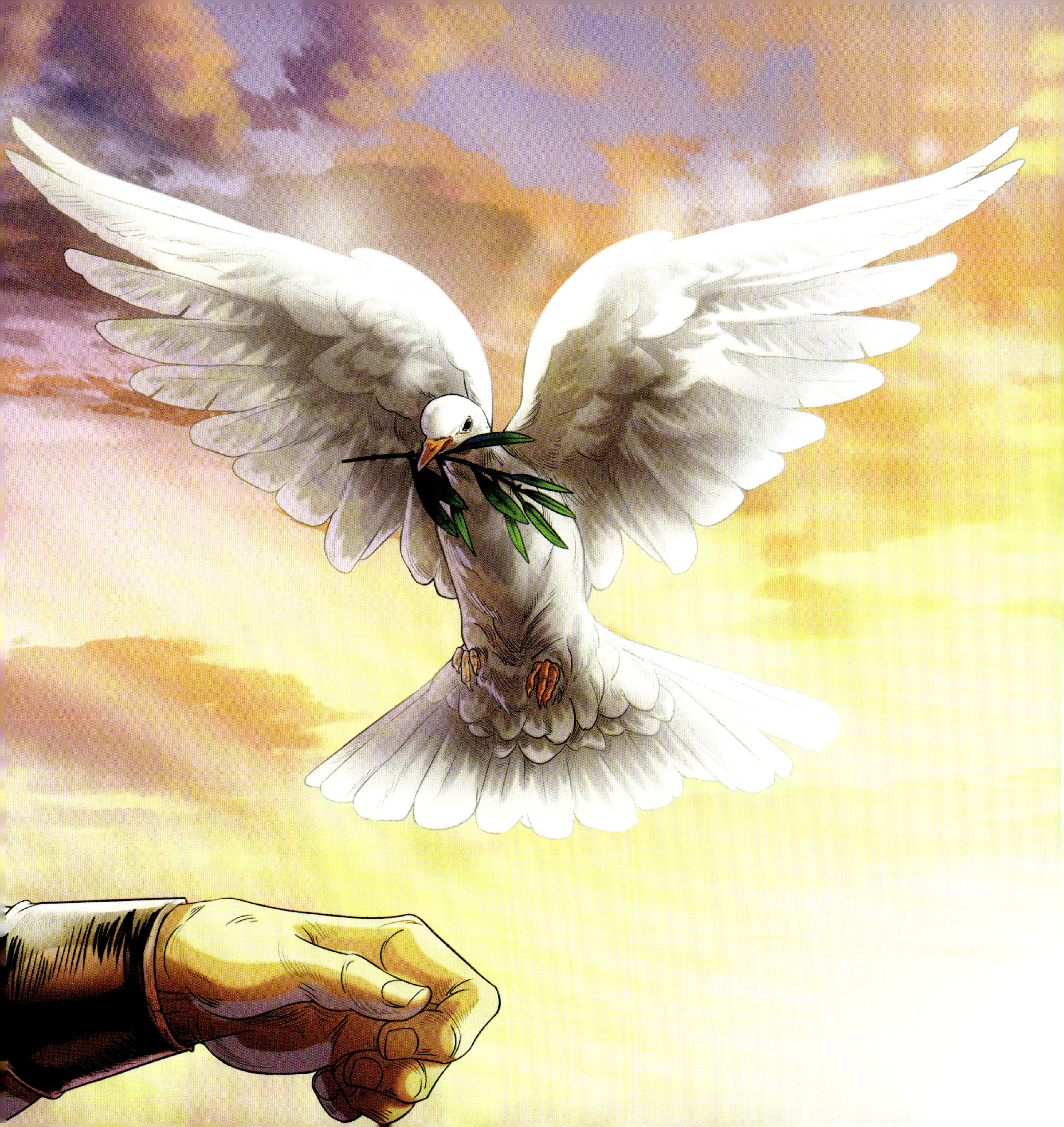

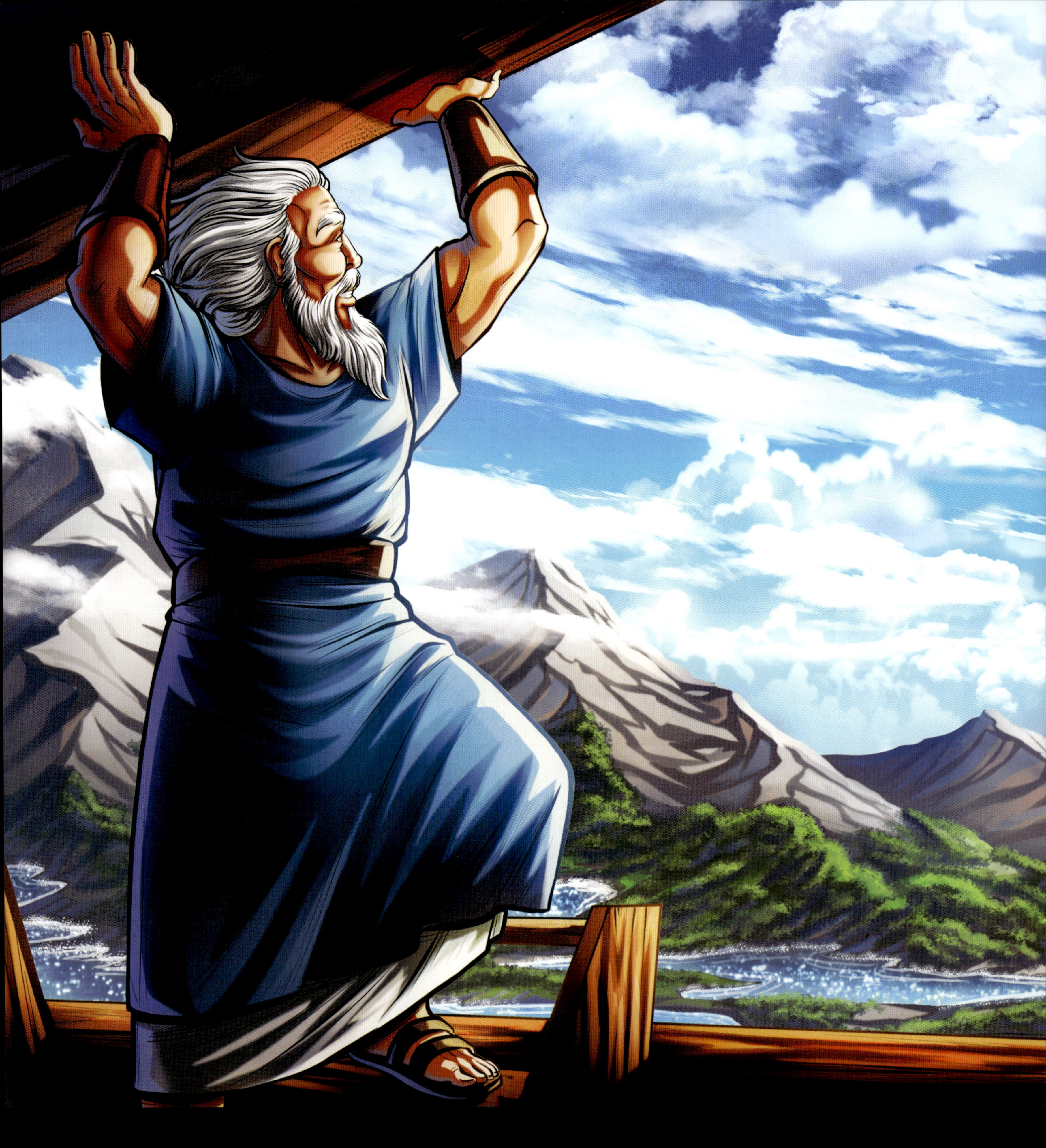

Noah waited another seven days and sent out the dove, only this time she did not return.

And Noah removed the covering of the ark and looked out and saw that the surface of the ground was dry.

THE GREAT FLOOD (PART 2) 49

After a year on the ark, God spoke to Noah, saying:

GOD: *Come out from the ark—you and your wife, and your sons, and their wives. Bring forth every beast, all the cattle, every bird, and everything that creeps on the ground, that they may multiply and replenish the earth.*

THE GREAT FLOOD (PART 2)

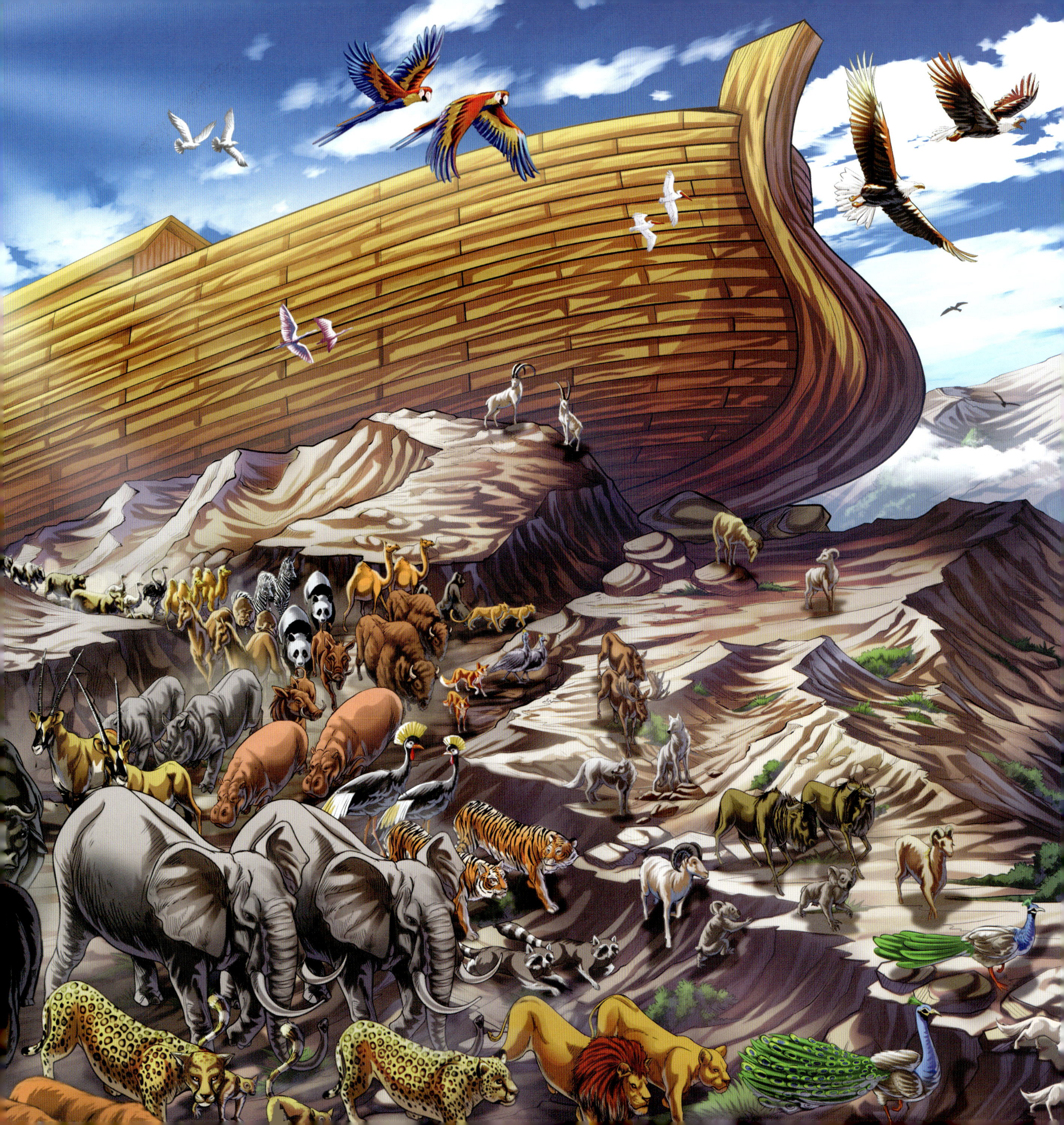

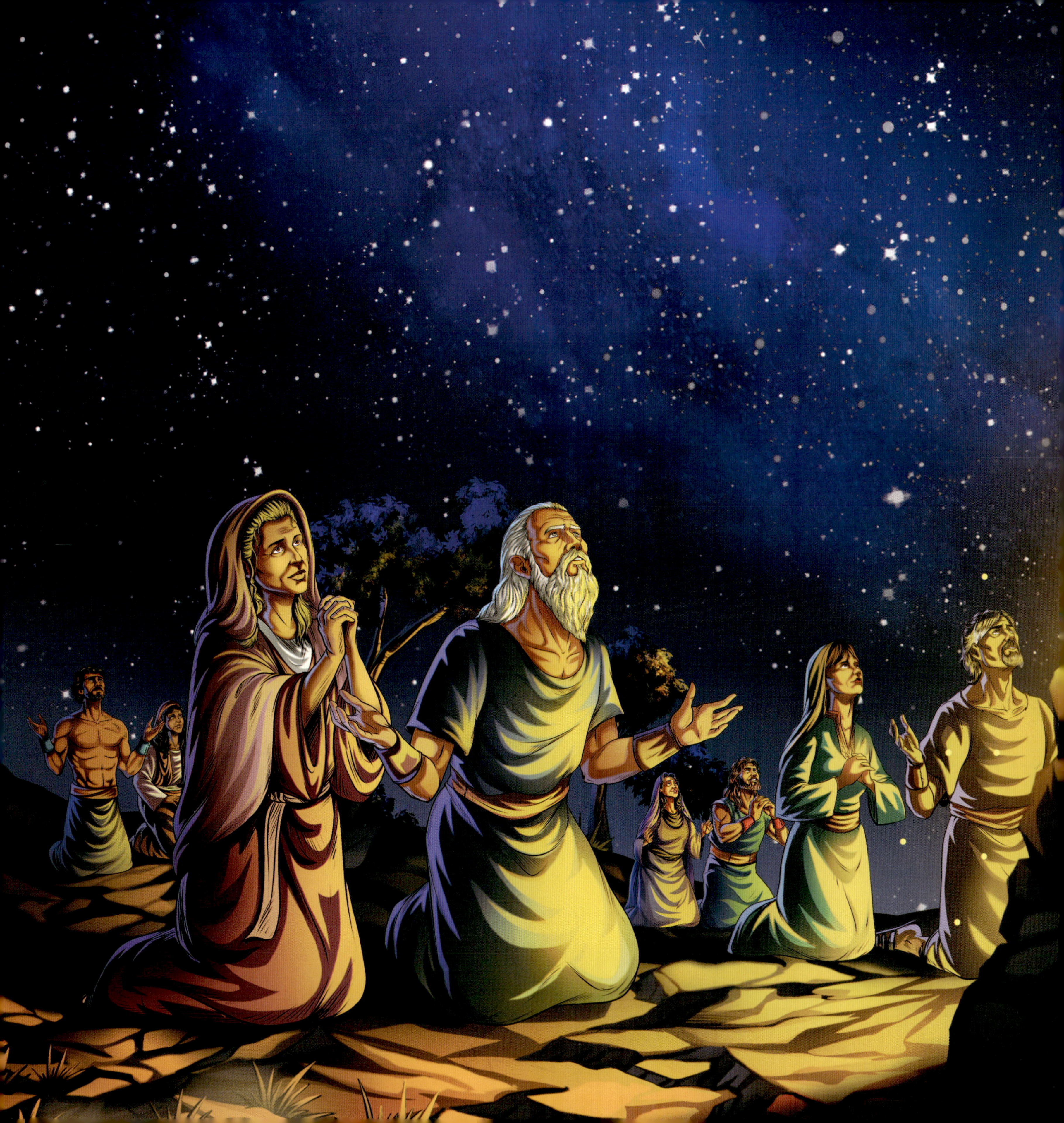

Then Noah built an altar to the LORD, and offered burnt offerings on the altar from every clean animal and every clean bird.

GOD: *I will never again curse the ground because of mankind, for the imaginations of man's heart is evil from his youth. I will never again destroy all living things as I have done.*

As long as the earth remains; planting and harvesting, summer and winter, and day and night will not cease.

THE GREAT FLOOD (PART 2) 55

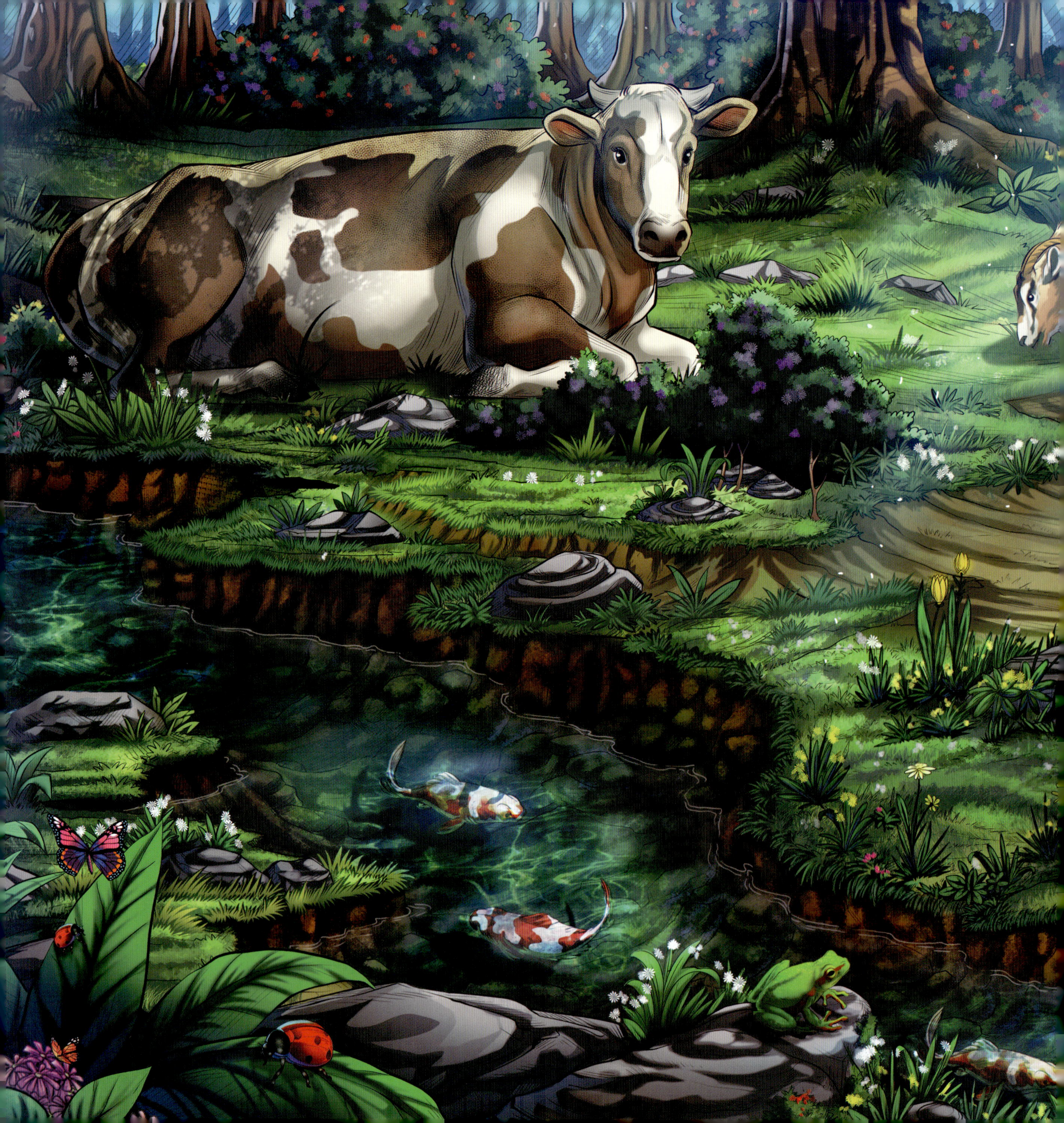

And the LORD God blessed Noah and his sons:

GOD: *Be fruitful and multiply and replenish the earth. Every beast of the earth, every fowl of the air, every creature on the ground, and all the fish of the sea will now fear you. I hand them over to you. Every living thing that moves shall be food for you; just as I gave you green plants, now I give you everything.*

GOD: *Whoever sheds man's blood, by man shall his blood be shed, for God made mankind in His own image.*

Be fruitful and multiply. Fill the earth and multiply on it.

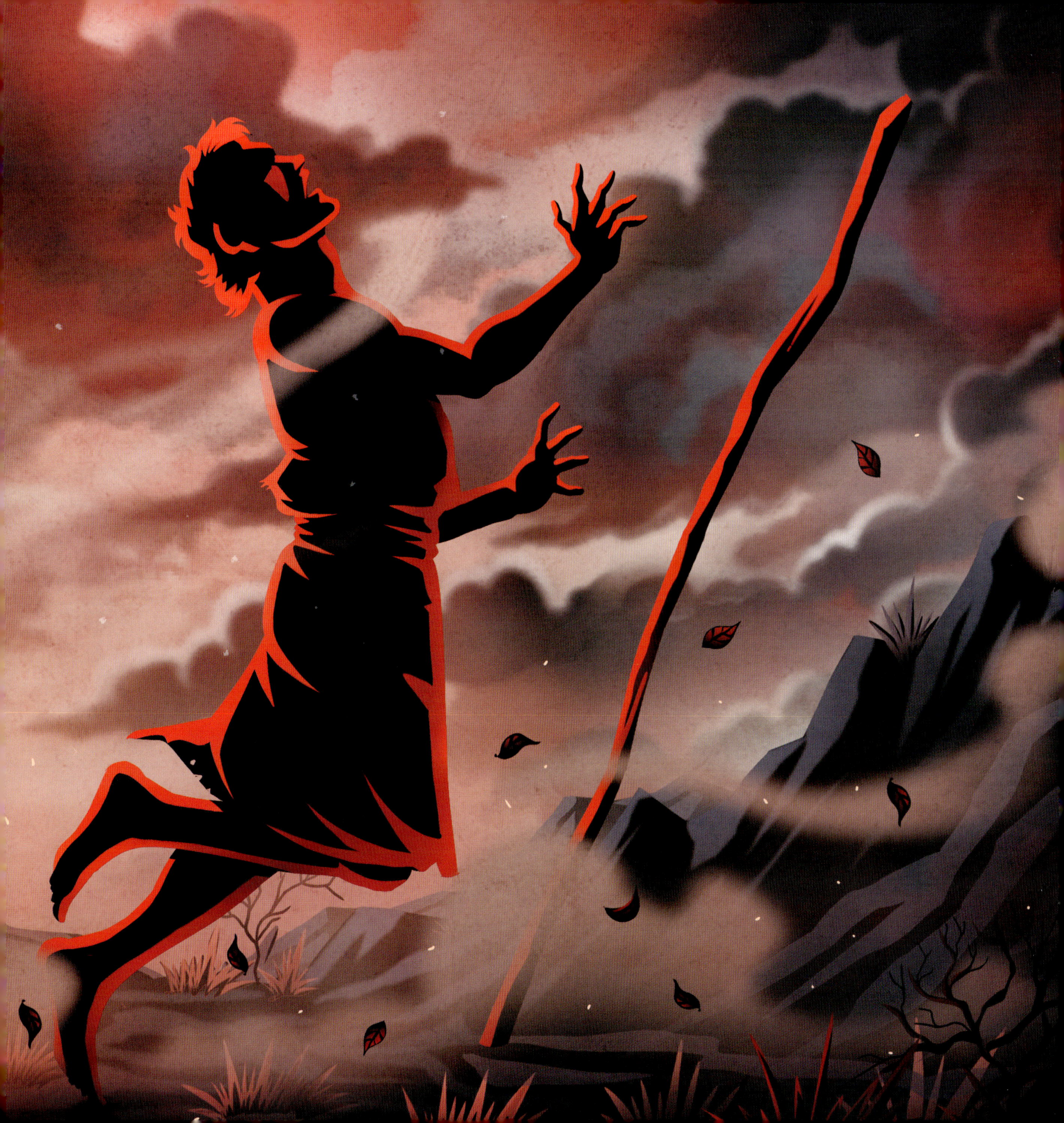

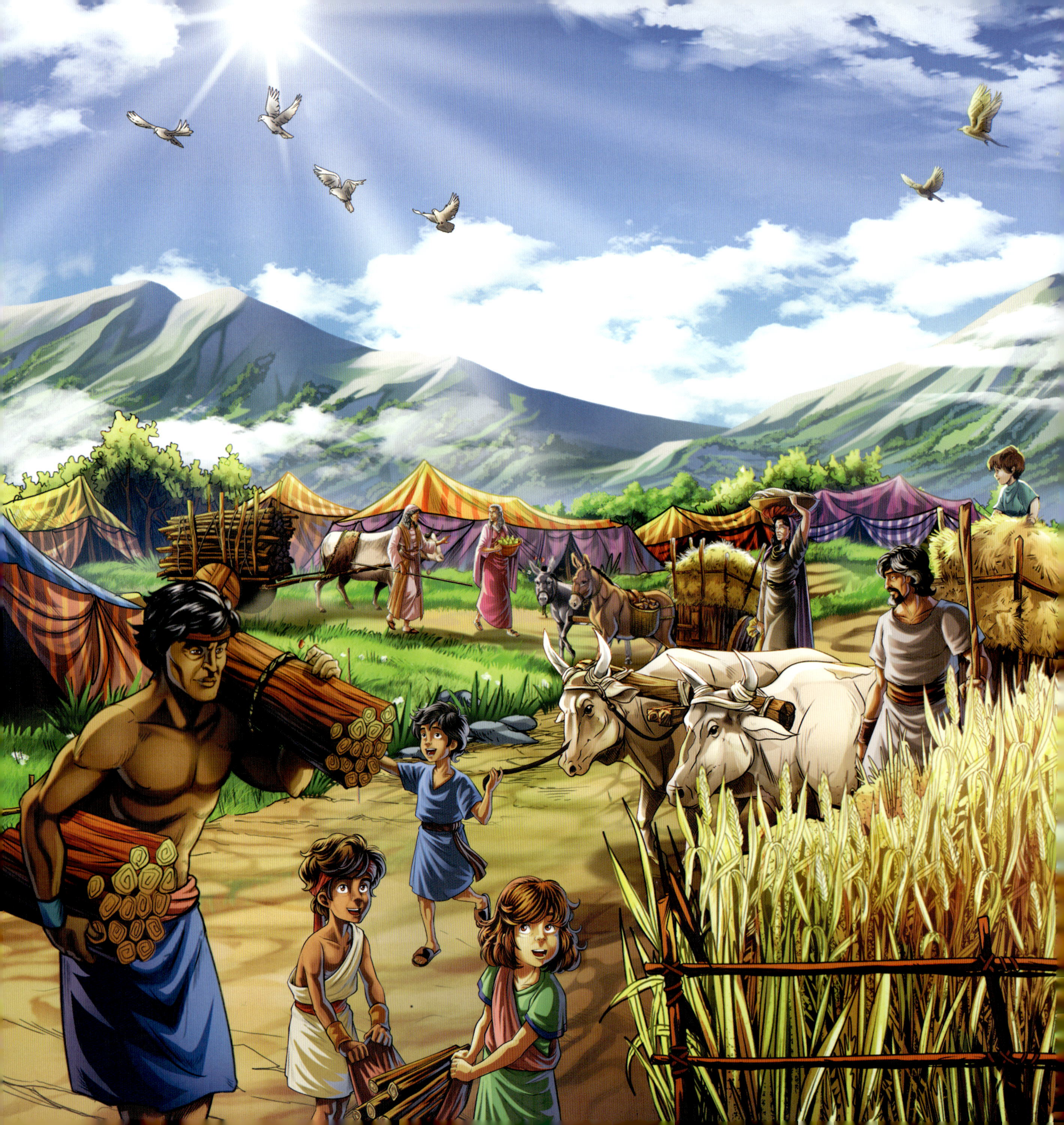

God spoke again to Noah and the sons who were with him:

GOD: *As for Me, I am establishing My covenant with you, with your descendants after you, and with every living creature that came out of the ark with you: every living creature of the earth. I will establish My covenant with you that never again will all living beings be destroyed by a flood. Never again will there be a flood to destroy the earth.*

THE GREAT FLOOD (PART 2) | 61

GOD: *This is the sign of My covenant I am making between Myself and you and every living creature for all generations to come: I have set My bow in the cloud, and it will be a sign of the covenant between Me and the earth. Whenever I bring clouds over the earth, and the bow is seen in the clouds, I will remember My covenant which is between Me and you and every living creature: the waters will never again destroy all living beings.*

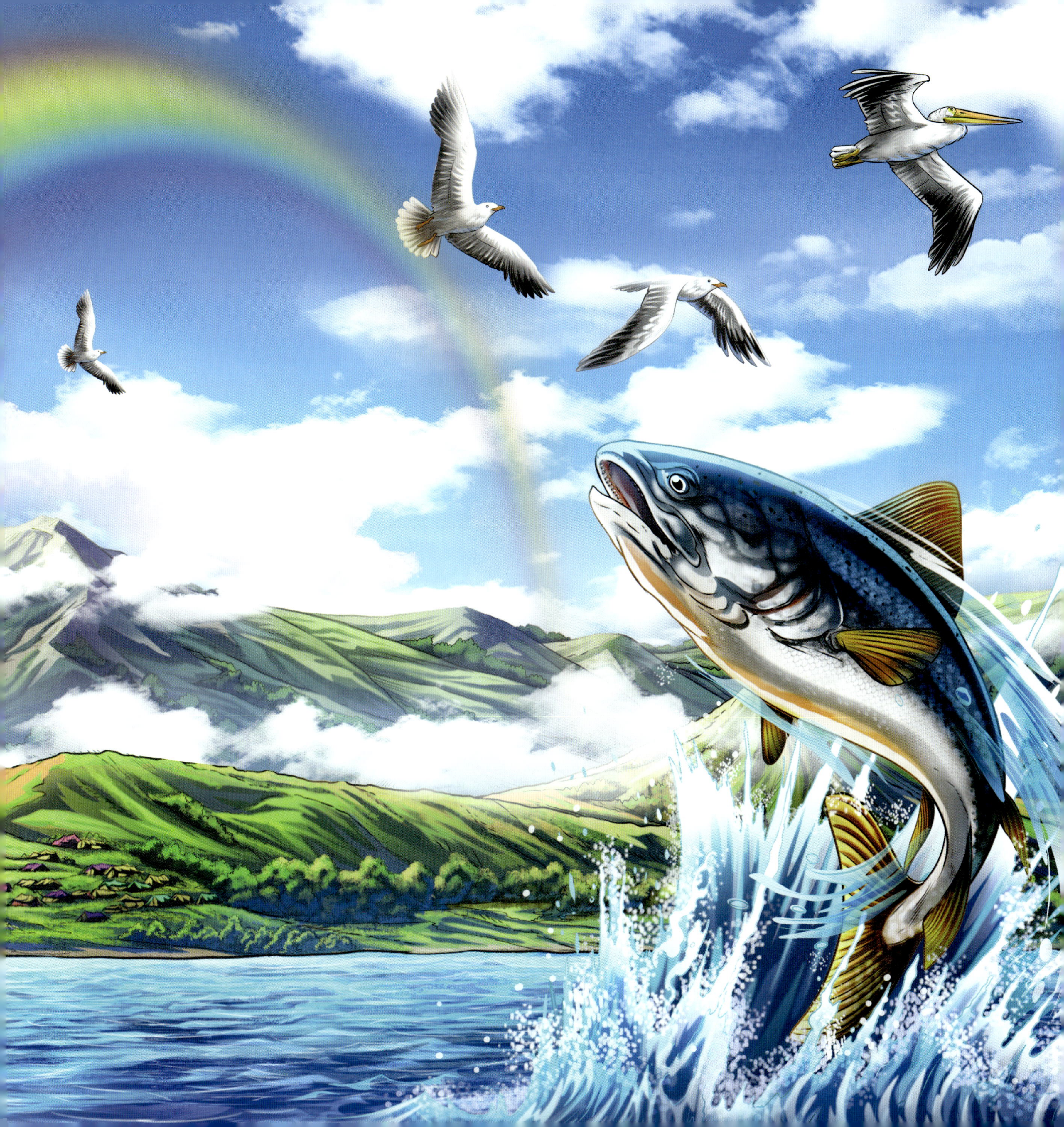

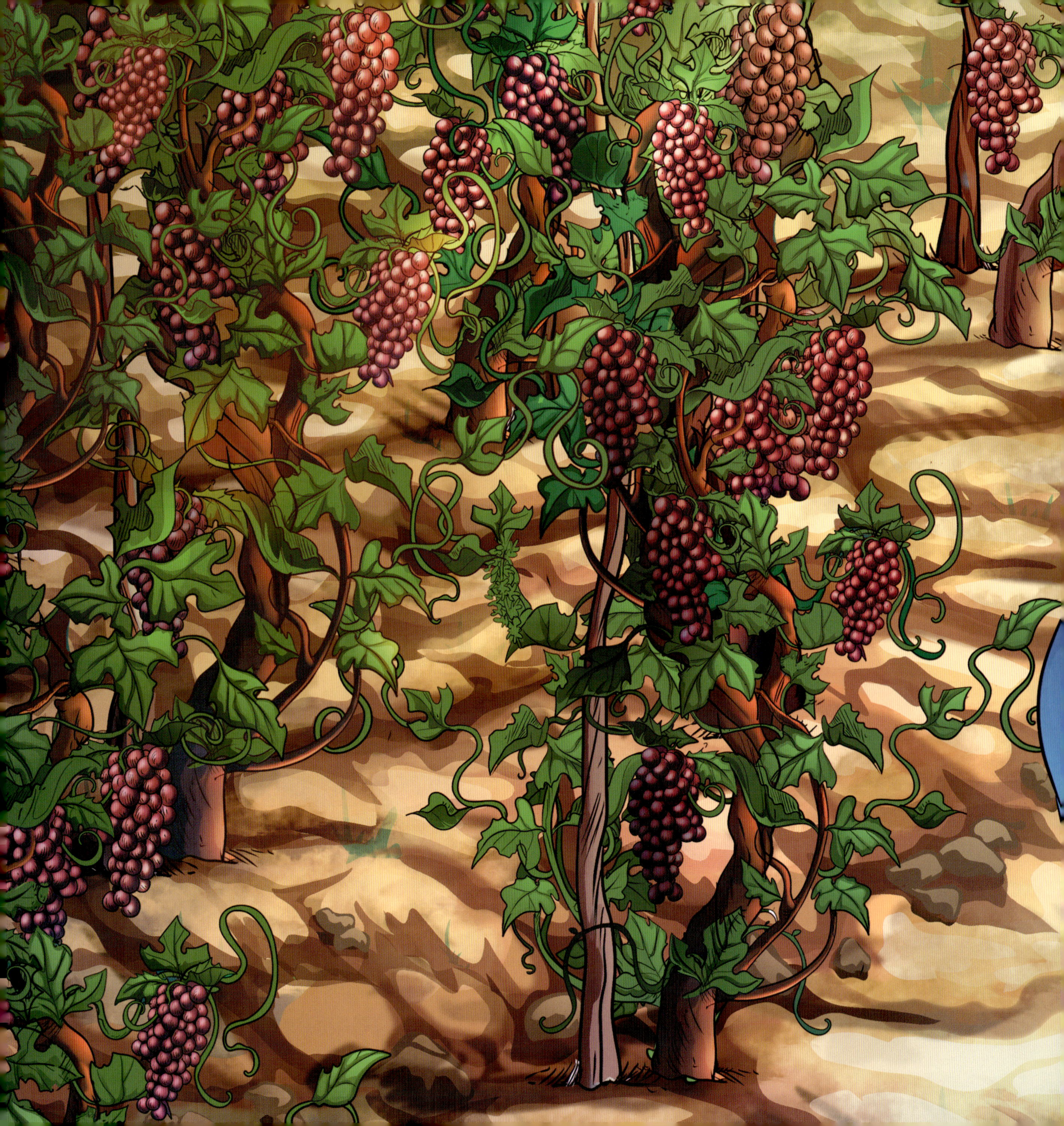

After the Great Flood, Noah began to work the ground and planted a vineyard. As his vineyard matured, Noah made wine from the grapes he had planted.

And one day, after drinking the wine, Noah became drunk, falling asleep naked in his tent.

THE GREAT FLOOD (PART 2)

Noah's youngest son, Ham, looked upon his father's nakedness, and went out to tell his two brothers what he had seen.

However, Ham's older brothers refused to look at their father's nakedness, and proceeded to walk backwards into their father's tent with a garment to cover his naked body. Their faces were turned away, so they did not see their father's shame.

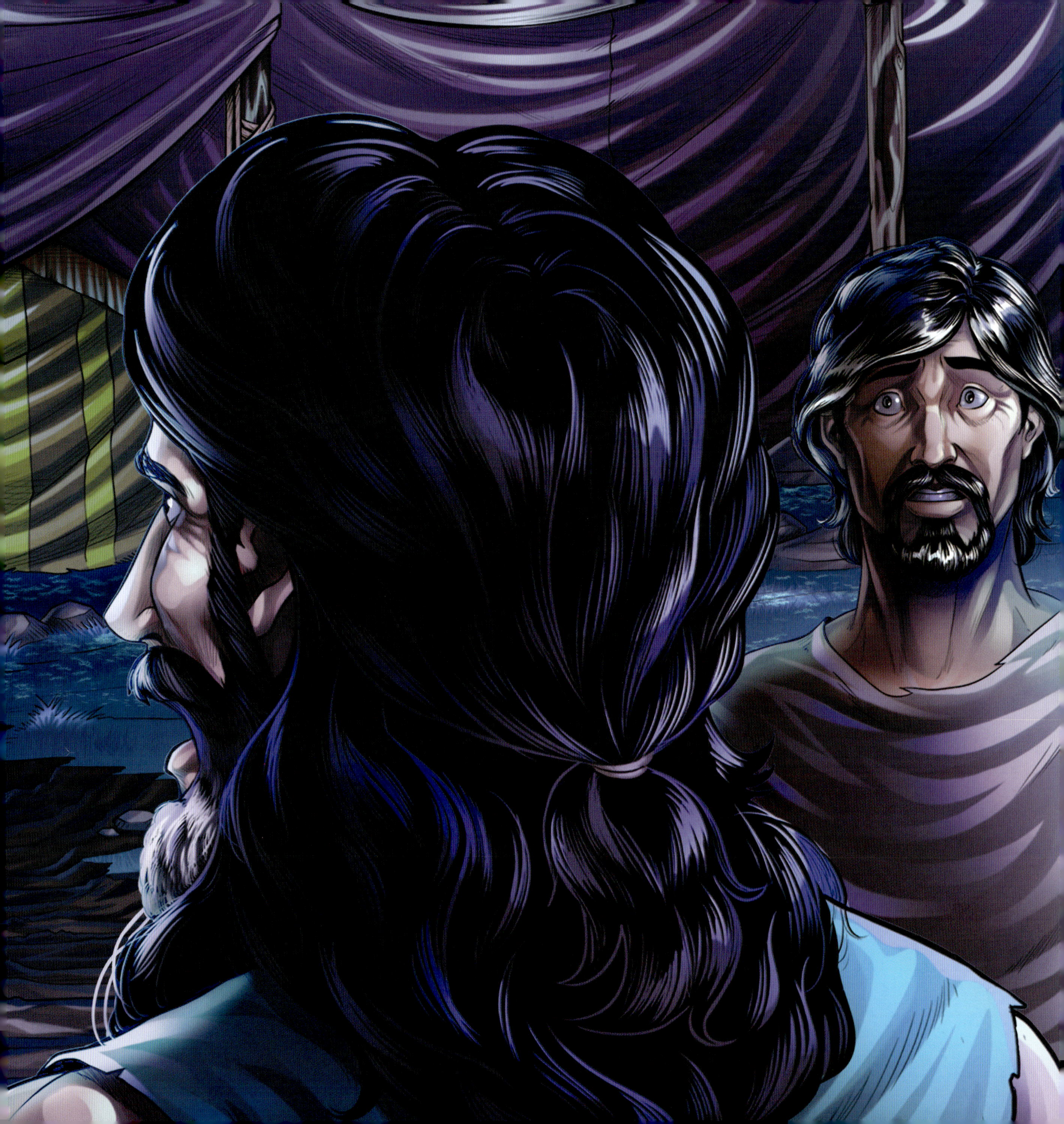

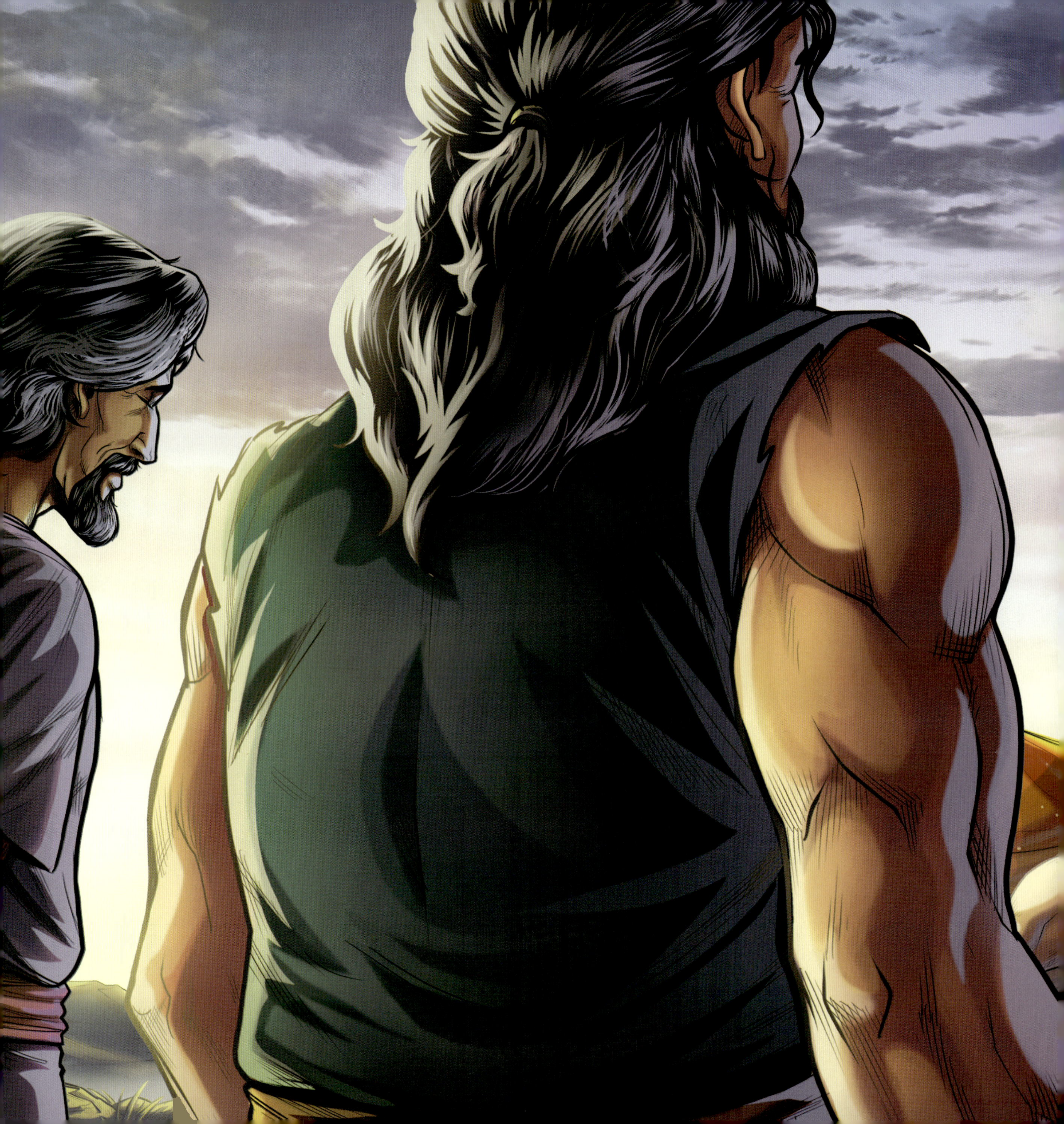

When Noah woke up from his drunken state and learned what Ham had done, he cursed Ham's youngest son Canaan.

NOAH: *Cursed be Canaan! A servant of servants he shall be to his brothers. Blessed be the LORD God of Shem, and let Canaan be his servant. May God enlarge Japheth and let him dwell in the tents of Shem, and let Canaan be his servant.*

THE GREAT FLOOD (PART 2) | 69

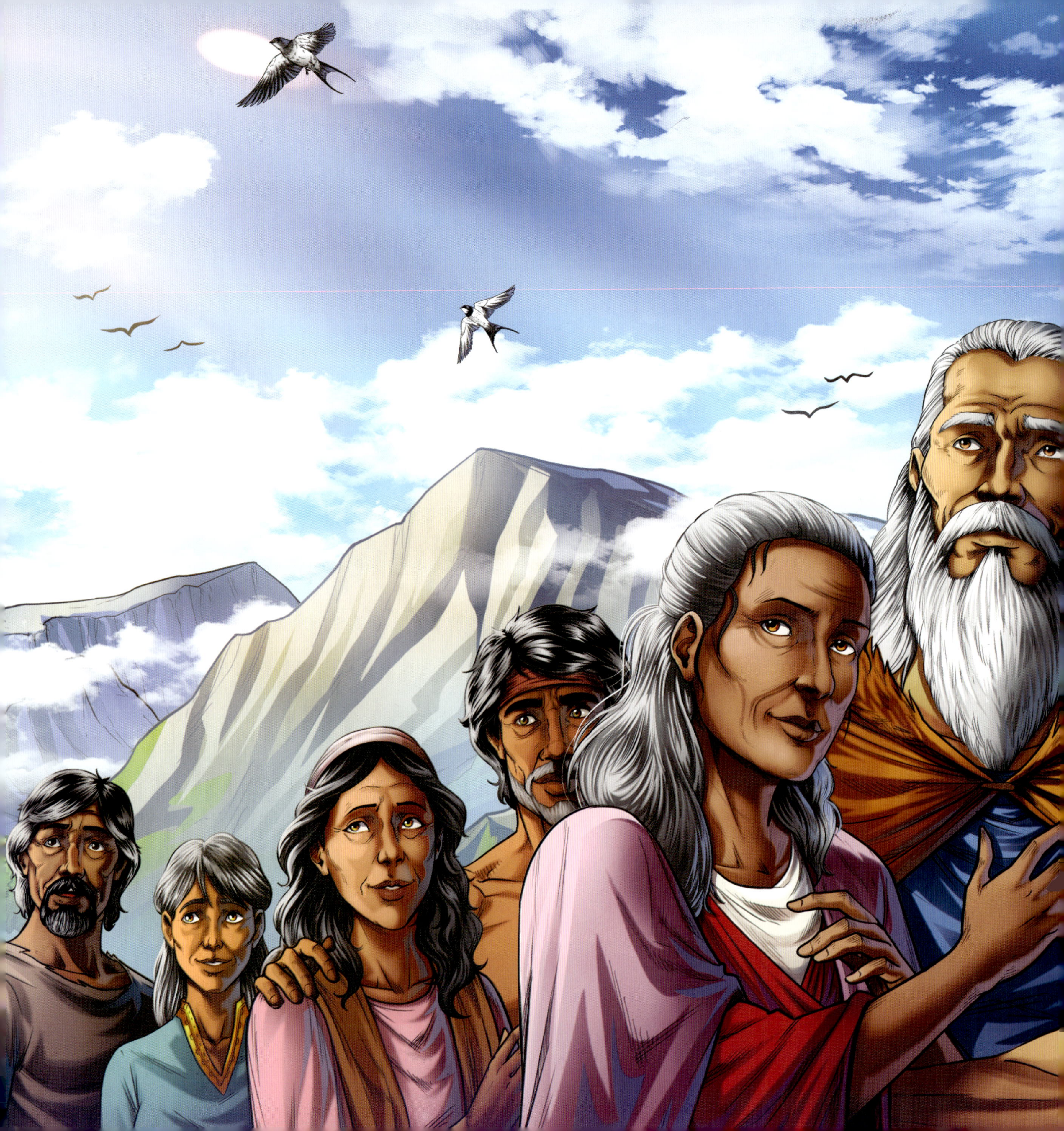

The sons of Noah that went forth from the ark were Shem, Ham, and Japheth. These three were the sons of Noah, and the whole earth was populated by them.

After the flood, Noah lived 350 years. All the days of Noah were 950 years, and then he died.

THE GREAT FLOOD (PART 2) | 71

Chapter 5: Key Scriptures

As for you, be fruitful and increase in number; multiply on the earth and increase upon it.

I have set my rainbow in the clouds, and it will be the sign of the covenant between me and the earth. Whenever I bring clouds over the earth and the rainbow appears in the clouds, I will remember my covenant between me and you and all living creatures of every kind. Never again will the waters become a flood to destroy all life.

—Genesis 9:7, 13–15

WATCH CHAPTER 5

CHAPTER 6:

The Tower of Babel

After the Great Flood, the sons of Noah and their wives began to repopulate the earth.

And among their descendants was a mighty man, a leader among men and a fierce hunter before the LORD.

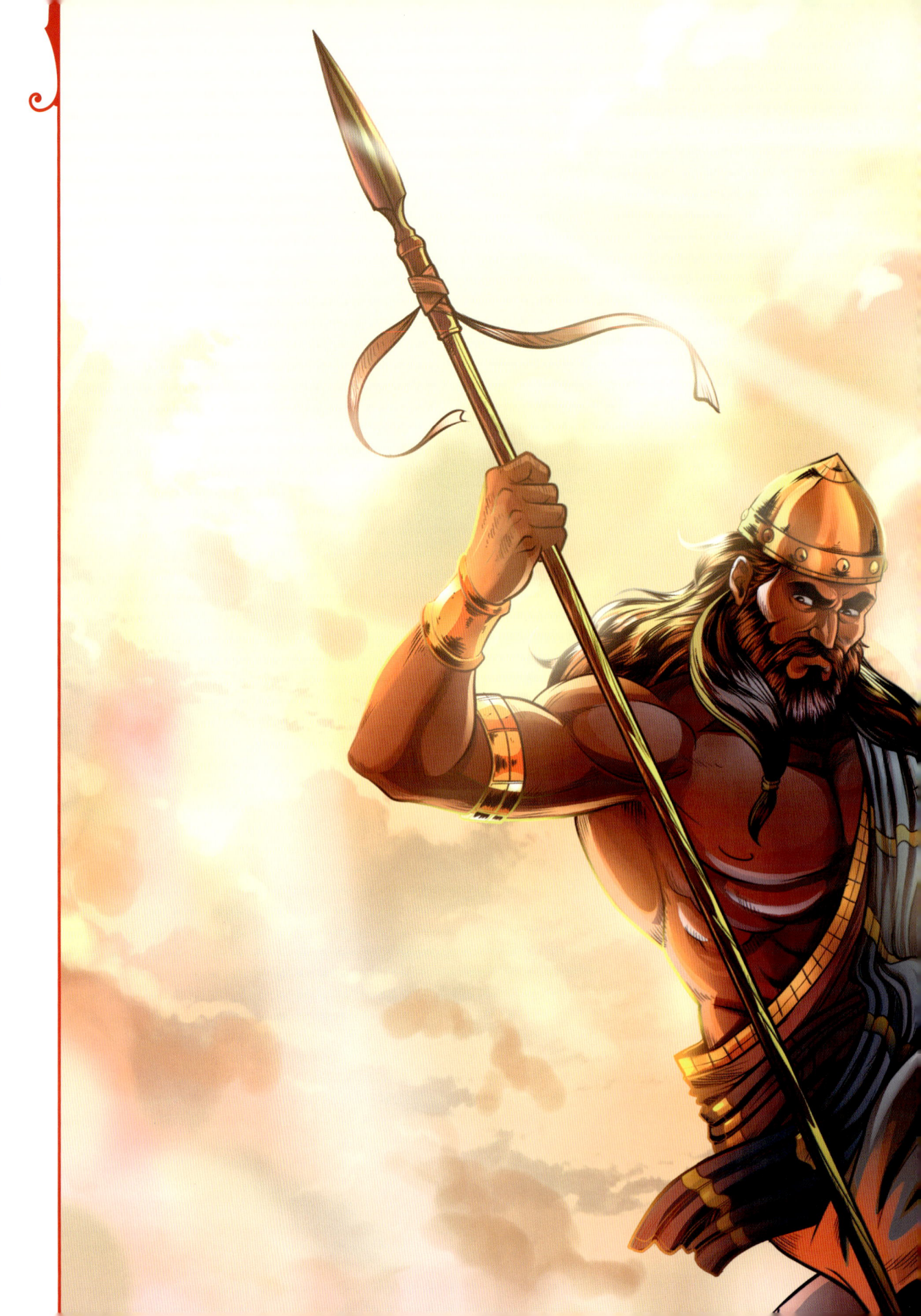

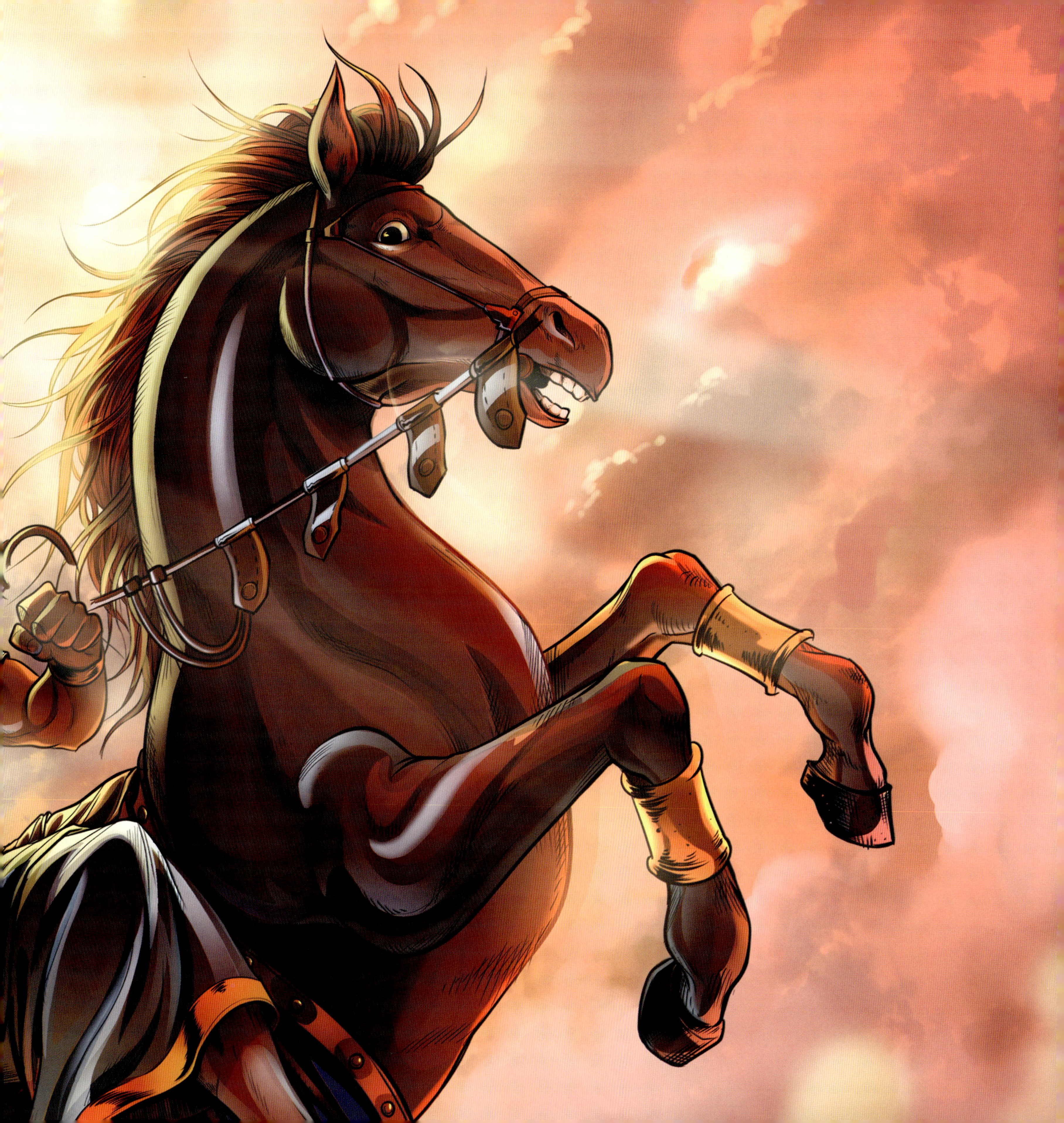

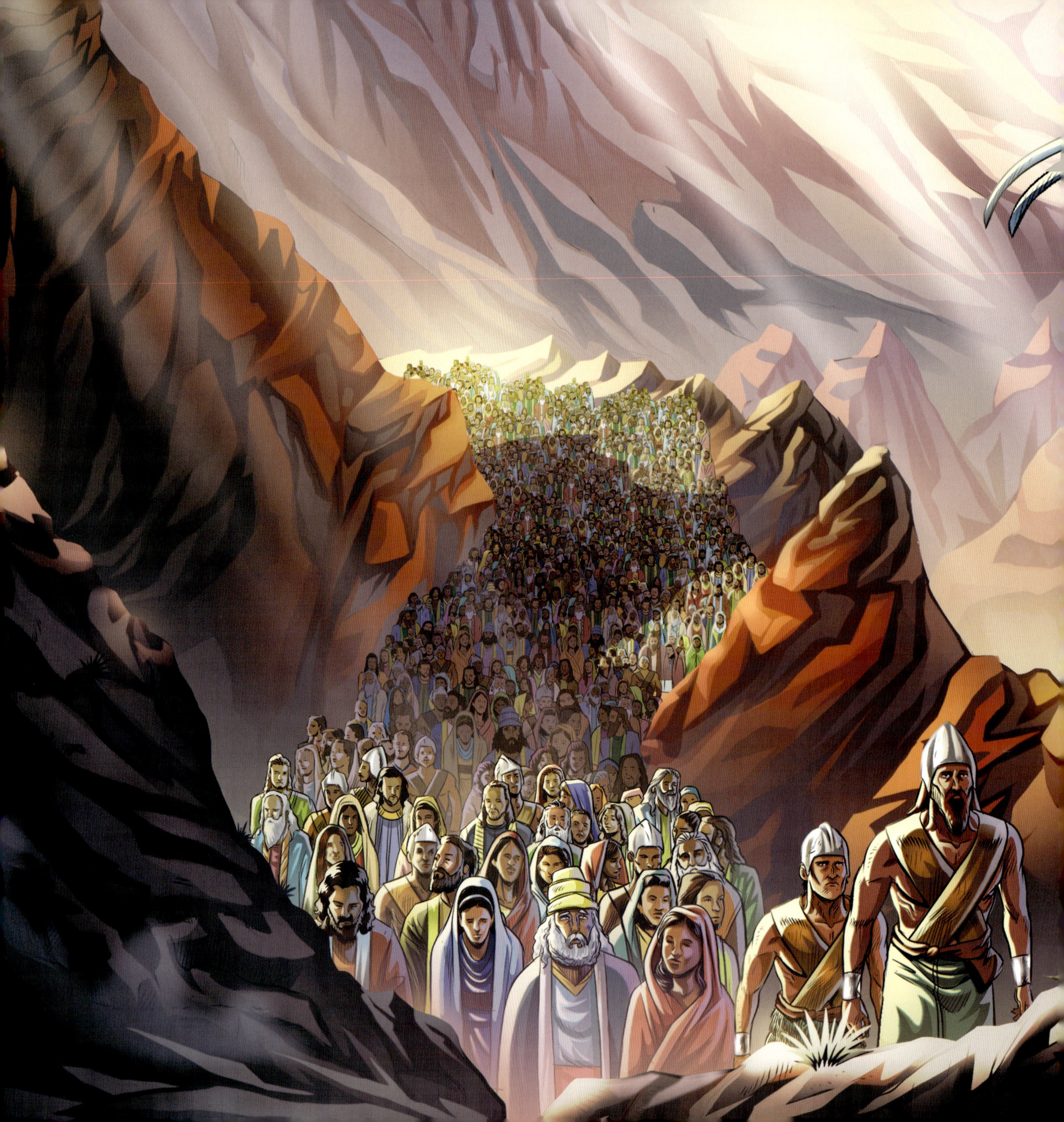

His name was Nimrod, and he was the great grandson of Noah through his son Ham and Ham's son Cush. And the beginnings of his kingdom included Babel in the land of Shinar.

At that time, the people of the earth spoke one language.

THE TOWER OF BABEL

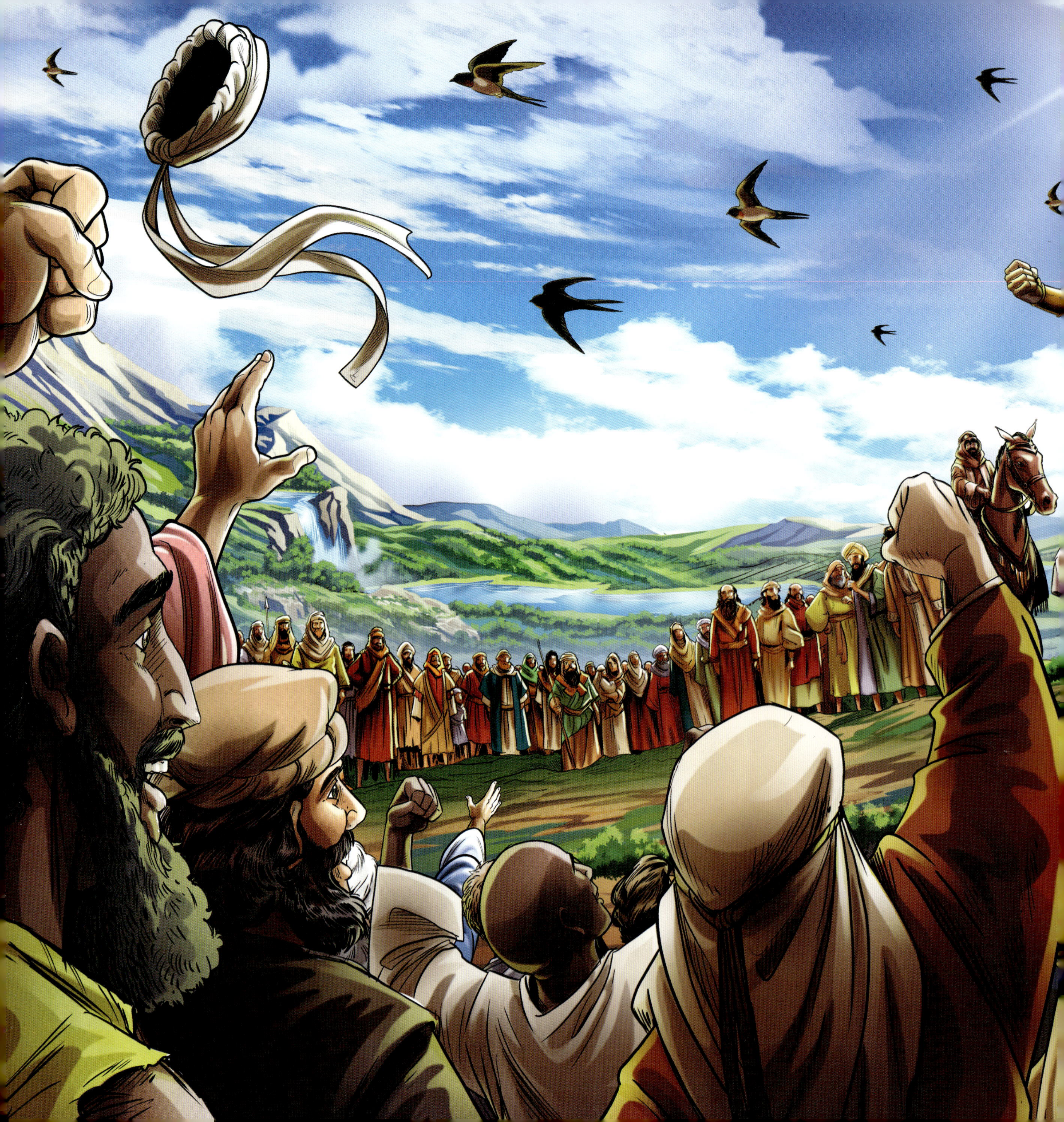

And as it came to pass, they traveled from the east, and found a plain in the land of Shinar and settled there, desiring to make a name for themselves.

THE TOWER OF BABEL | 79

NIMROD: *With bricks and mortar we shall build a great city! And in our city, we will build a tower with its top reaching up into the heavens! We shall settle here. We shall not be scattered all over the face of the earth.*

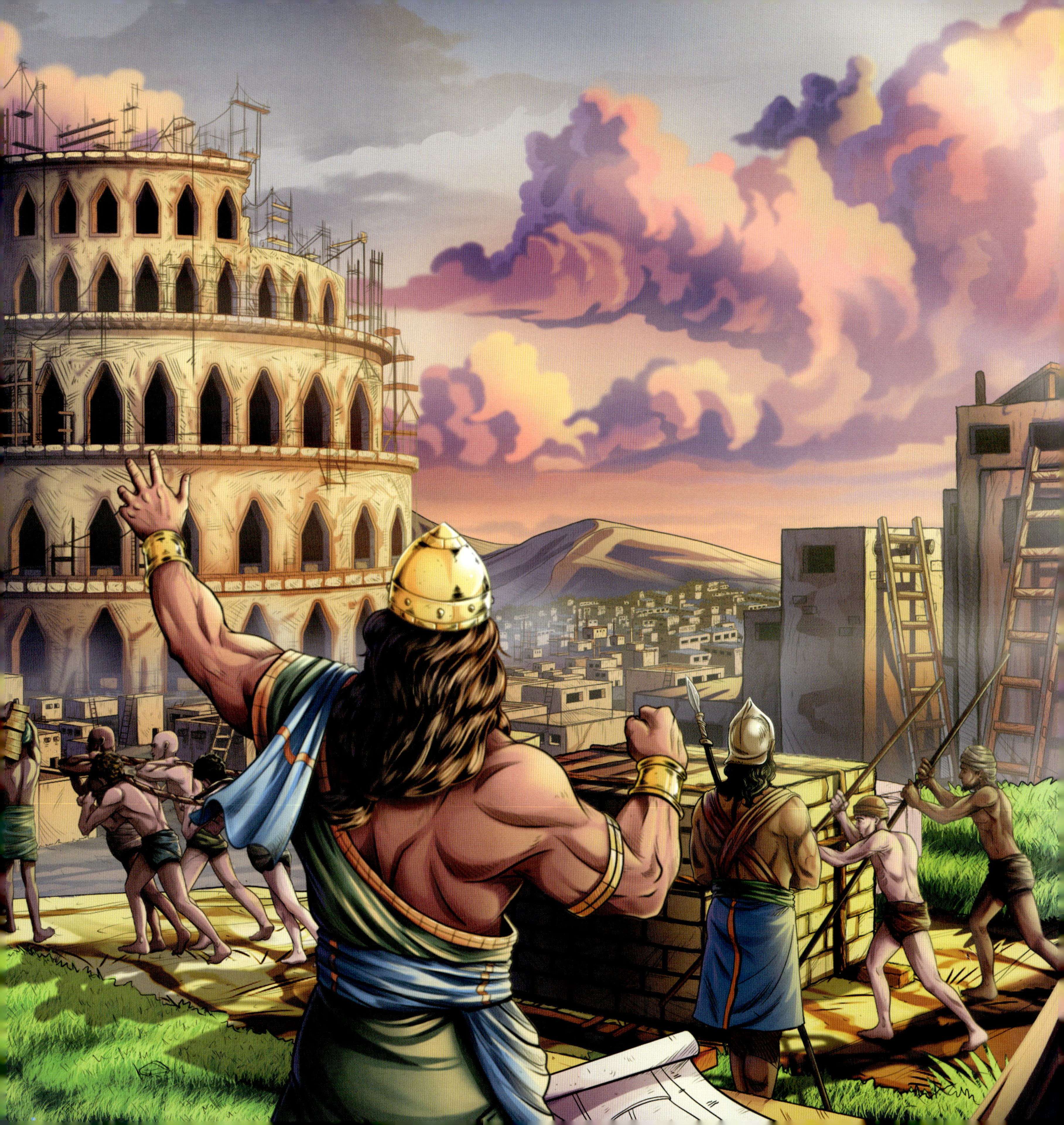

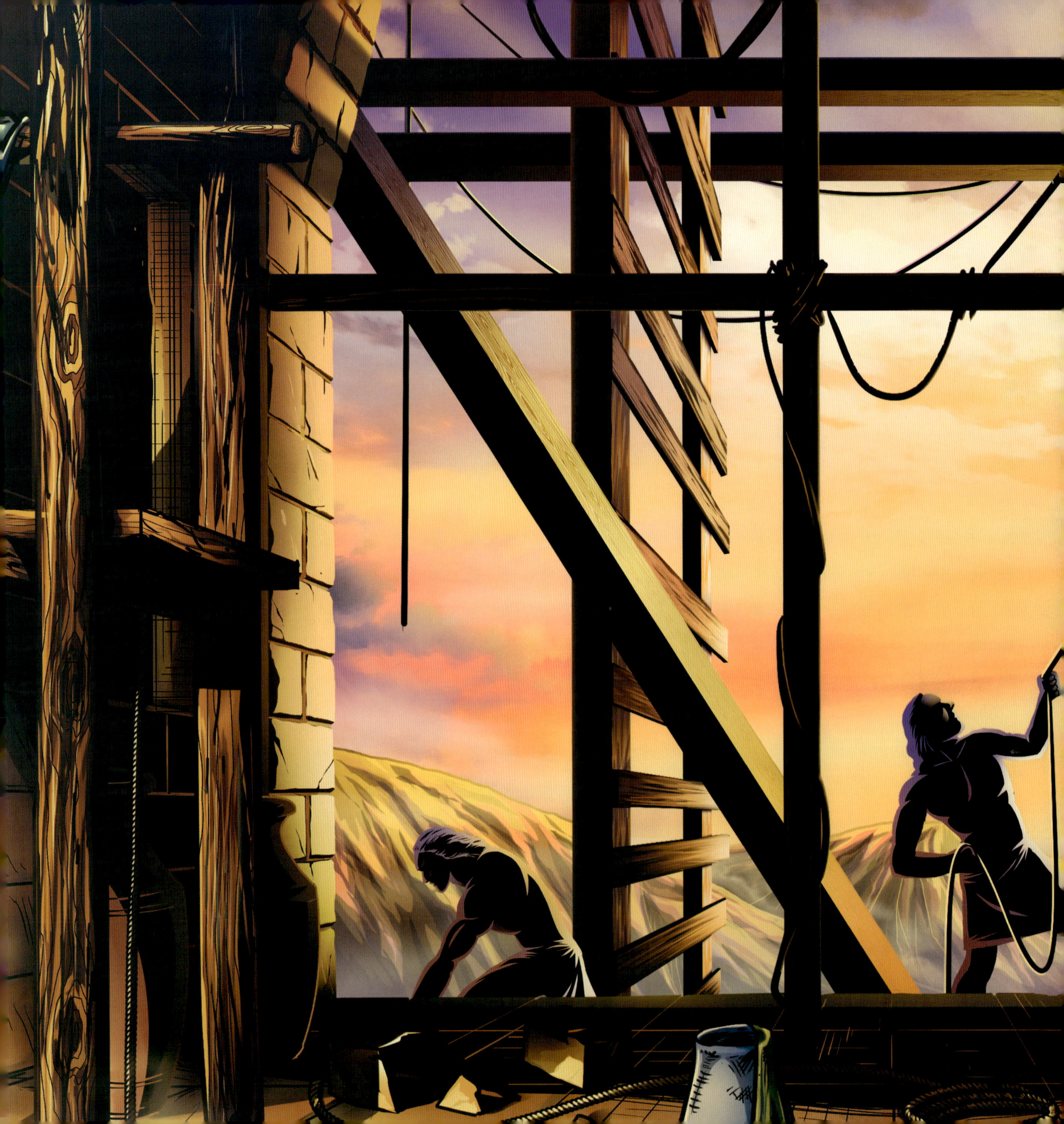

As the people continued to build, the LORD came down to see their city and their tower.

THE TOWER OF BABEL 83

And the LORD said:

GOD: Behold, the people are united, and they all share one language, and this is what they have started to do. Now nothing they set out to accomplish will be impossible for them.

THE TOWER OF BABEL | 84

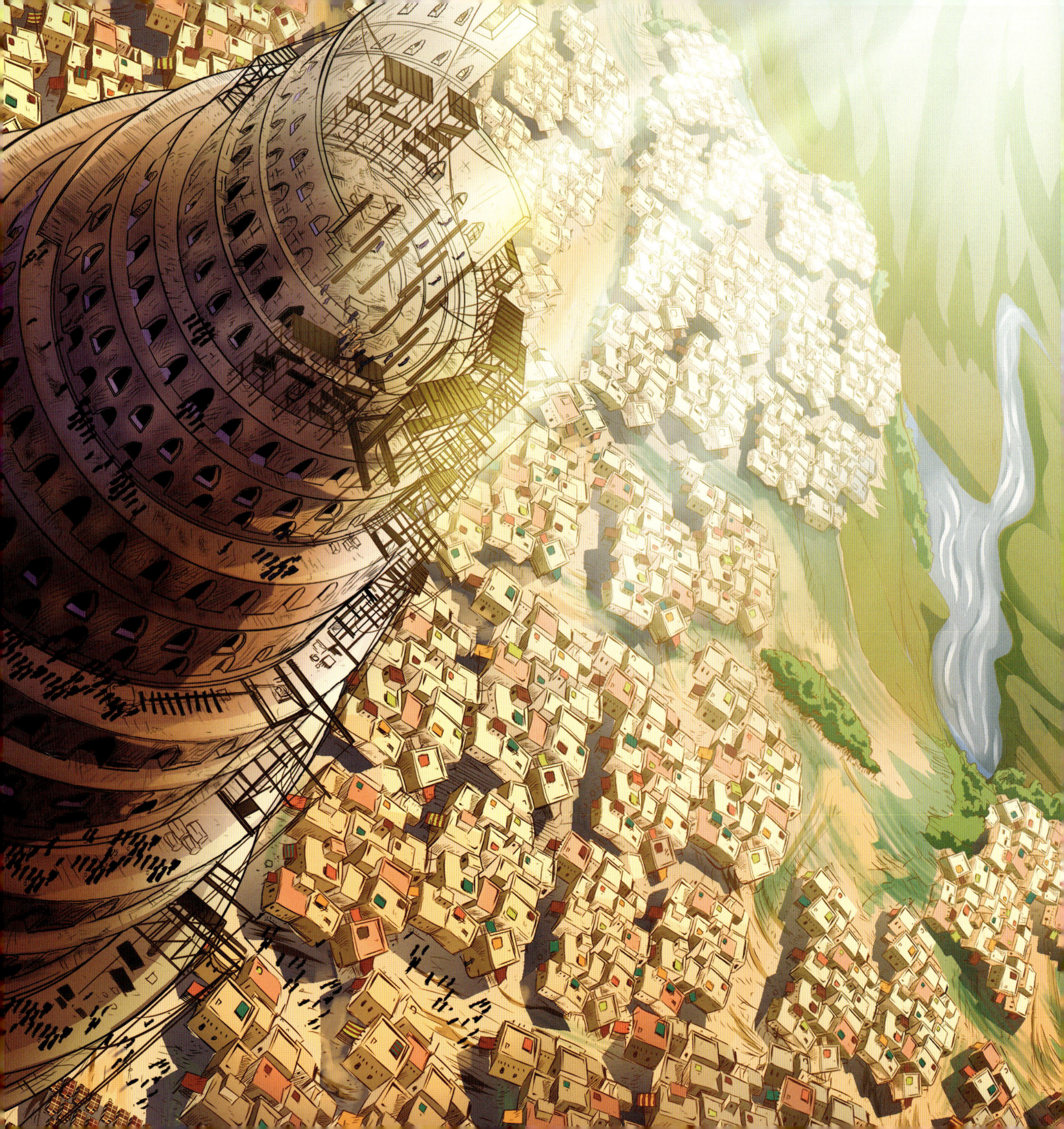

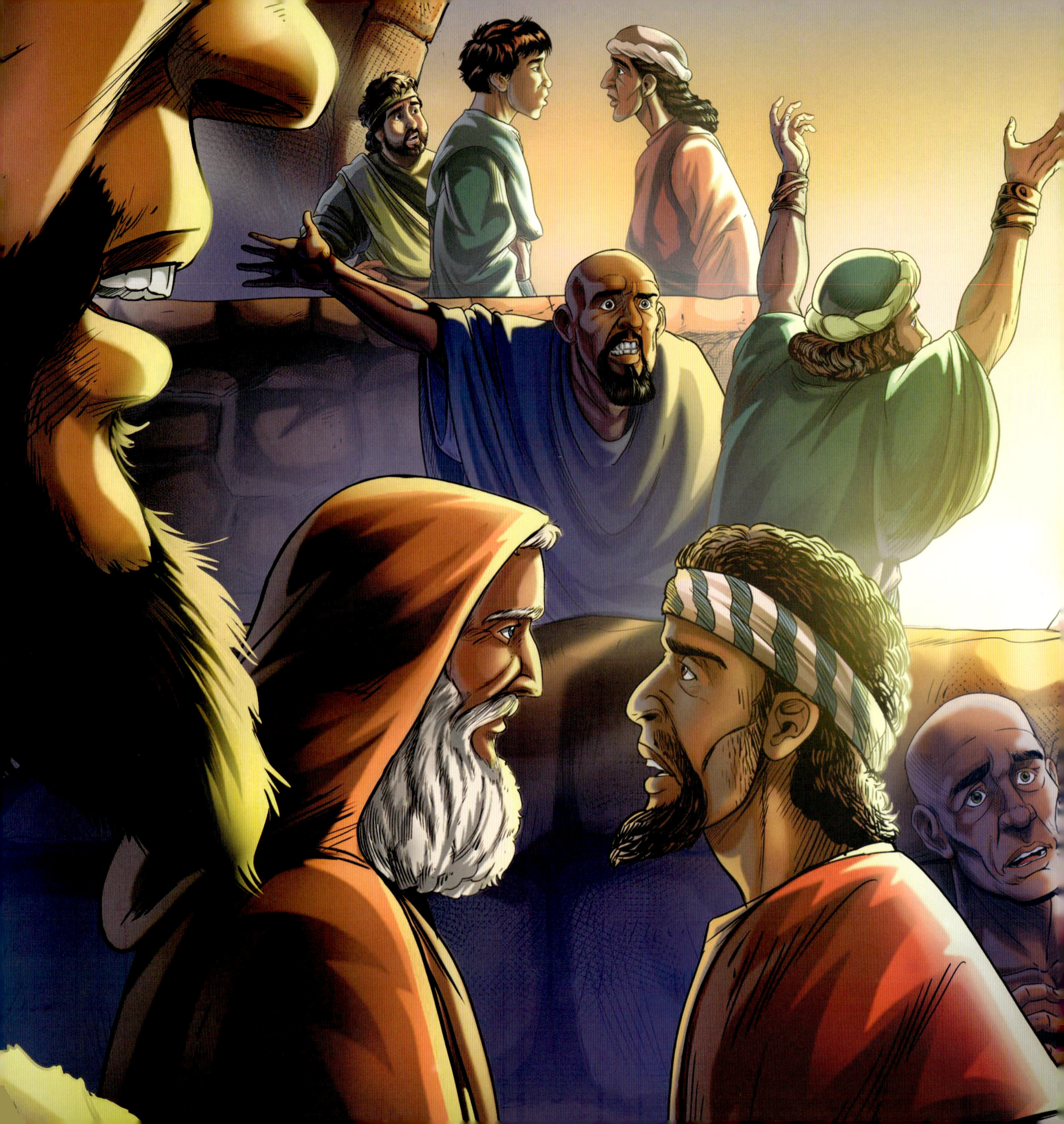

GOD: *Come, let Us go down and confuse their language, so they might not understand one another's speech.*

THE TOWER OF BABEL | 87

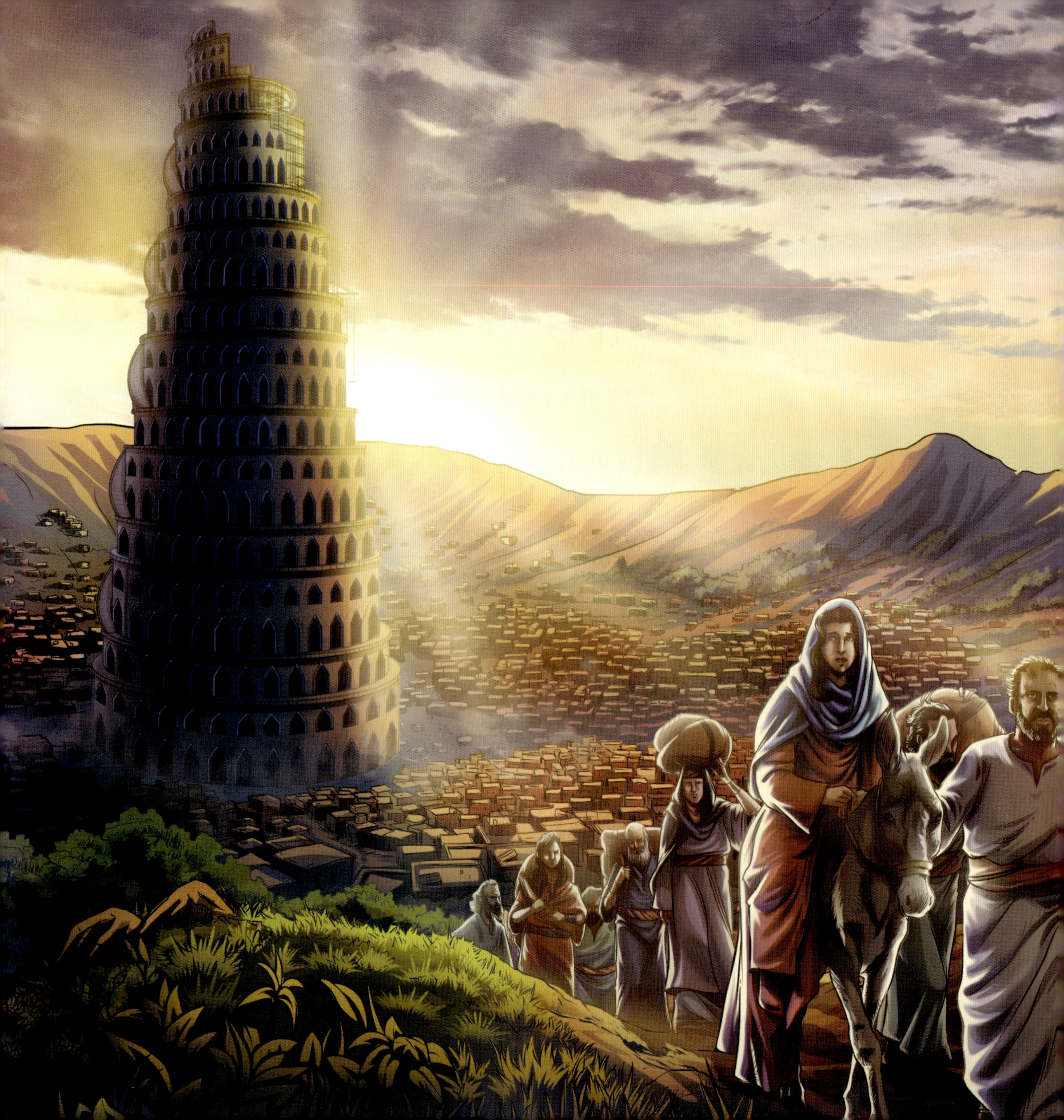

So, the LORD scattered the people all over the earth, and the building of the city and the tower stopped.

Therefore, its name was called "Babel" because it was there God confused their language and scattered the people over the face of the earth.

Chapter 6: Key Scriptures

Then they said, "Come, let us build ourselves a city, with a tower that reaches to the heavens, so that we may make a name for ourselves; otherwise we will be scattered over the face of the whole earth."

[The Lord said], "Come, let us go down and confuse their language so they will not understand each other." So the Lord scattered them from there over all the earth, and they stopped building the city.

—Genesis 11:4, 7–8

WATCH CHAPTER 6

iBIBLE Storybook Volume 3

Follow along with the Biblical narrative as Abram is called by God out of the land of Ur to follow Him to the land of promise, and as God makes a promise to make Abram a father of many nations.

See the faithfulness of God throughout Abram's story of waiting for his promised child. **iBIBLE Storybook Volume 3** includes Chapters 7-10: The Call of Abram; The Kings' War; Abram to Abraham; and Lot, Sodom & Gomorrah.

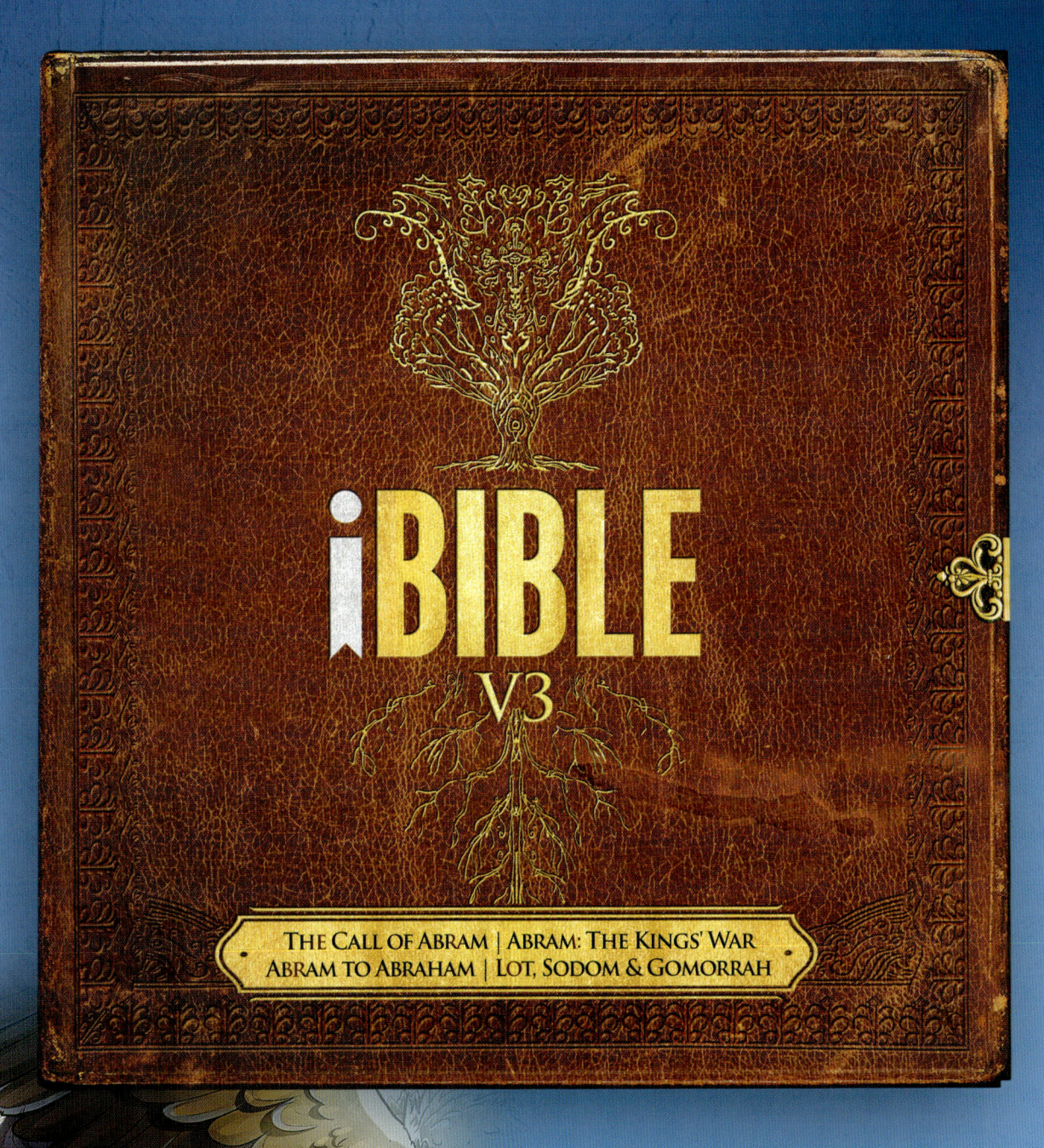

Animated episodes of each chapter are available as they are completed at **www.i.BIBLE**.

Seth

Enos

Cainan

Mahalaleel

Jared

Enoch

Methuselah

Lamech

Cush

Ham

Noah

Nimrod

The Great Flood

1. The sons of God take wives as they please.
2. The Nephilim are on the earth.
3. God sees that the people on earth are very wicked.
4. God speaks to Noah and tells him about the flood.
5. Noah makes the ark that God instructs him to make.
6. Animals are gathered into the ark.
7. The flood overpowers the earth.
8. After 150 days, the boat comes to rest on Mount Ararat.

The Tower of Babel

9. Noah, his family, and all the animals leave the ark.
10. Noah builds an altar to the LORD and offers burnt offerings.
11. God sets his rainbow in the clouds as a sign of the covenant.
12. Noah plants a vineyard and becomes drunk.
13. Nimrod desires to build a great city and a tower.
14. The people build the tower.
15. God comes down and confuses their language.
16. The LORD scatters the people all over the earth.

RM
REVELATIONMEDIA

www.i.BIBLE